Ted Alan Studebaker

Ted Alan Studebaker

An Enduring Force for Peace

GARY W. STUDEBAKER

and

DOUGLAS E. STUDEBAKER

Foreword by Bill Herod

RESOURCE *Publications* · Eugene, Oregon

TED ALAN STUDEBAKER
An Enduring Force for Peace

Resource Publications
An Imprint of Wipf and Stock Publishers
199 W. 8th Ave., Suite 3
Eugene, OR 97401

www.wipfandstock.com

PAPERBACK ISBN: 978-1-5326-1703-4
HARDCOVER ISBN: 978-1-4982-8748-7
EBOOK ISBN: 978-1-4982-4141-0

Manufactured in the U.S.A.   FEBRUARY 12, 2026

Contents

Foreword

TED STUDEBAKER WAS AN active pacifist, a committed Christian and a courageous peacemaker whose faith led him to put his life on the line in wartime Vietnam.

Ted was also my friend and colleague. We were both conscientious objectors who opposed U.S. policy in Vietnam, and we were both volunteers through the Church of the Brethren serving as civilian development workers with Vietnam Christian Service (VNCS).

Like the poor villagers with whom we worked, we were non-combatants, but we knew that in "modern" war most casualties are non-combatants.

Ted knew he was in a dangerous place at a dangerous time and he took simple precautions to protect himself and those around him while still being able to do the work he loved. He learned Vietnamese and the language of the Koho (an ethnic minority with whom he worked closely). He moved easily in the nearby villages while keeping his distance from military installations and personnel. The people around him saw that he had no weapons or communications equipment and that he lived in a house without guards or high walls.

Living in a war zone, however, it is impossible to inoculate oneself against the surrounding violence and Ted fell, an innocent victim of war, just like millions of others.

To those of us who knew Ted, however, his sacrifice holds a very special place in our hearts. Nearly half a century later we remember him with particular affection and respect.

All who lived in remote areas faced constant danger and knew it, but we all lived in joyful hope that someday the war would end and we could live in peace. Like Ted, we worked to prepare ourselves and those around us for that distant day.

When Ted was killed, I was out of contact, visiting the VNCS team in Dong Ha, another dangerous outpost. I made note of a poster they had on their wall. It was a poem by Lawrence Ferlinghetti, "The World is a Beautiful Place."

The next day I was in Da Nang and went to visit a VNCS staff person there. She had just received the word of Ted's death and told me. We both sat in stunned silence. Then I pulled out my notebook and read the last lines of Ferlinghetti's poem:

> "Yes
> but then right in the middle of it
> comes the smiling
> mortician."

And so it was with Ted's life. He had been married for one week following a romantic courtship, was doing wonderful work with people he loved and who loved him. His whole life was a beacon of hope in a landscape of death and destruction. He was doing everything right, "but then right in the middle of it comes the smiling mortician."

Faith doesn't promise success or even survival, but it does promise the opportunity to remain faithful and Ted was faithful to the end as the bullets smashed into his chest and he fell to the floor beneath his own anti-war poster in orange and black:

> Suppose They Gave a War
> . . . and Nobody Came

Those of us who knew Ted, work toward that day and we continue to live in joyful hope, the way forward illumined by his example.

Bill Herod
Mondulkiri, Cambodia
August 16, 2016

Preface

"Nonviolence is not for Wimps."

—RALPH DULL

THE WORK FOR PEACE and justice through nonviolence is the chosen pursuit of a small number of individuals and organizations around the world. This calls for advocating and educating the public. It sometimes means building trust while finding ways to bring some degree of economic progress to areas devastated by war, natural disaster or poverty. Working to build peace and justice are often pursued in underdeveloped countries through projects in such areas as education, agriculture, health care, construction, cultural preservation, language development, marketing, etc. Resourcefulness and perseverance are necessary to establish rapport, learn the local language, customs and to engage in projects that contribute to the well-being of the people being served.

People who work for peace through nonviolence often face resistance. Mahatma Gandhi said, "The path of true nonviolence requires much more courage than violence." Many of these courageous individuals are willing to relinquish their own personal liberties as they seek ways to contribute to the well-being of the people they live among. These volunteers include both well-known and lesser known individuals. The list is too extensive to include here, but some of these workers are: Dorothy Stang, Oscar Arias Sanchez, Malala Youfsafzai, Dietrich Bonhoeffer, Mohandas Gandhi, Martin Luther King Jr., Nelson Mandela and Ted Studebaker. Their stories portray selfless individuals who are willing to work to alleviate poverty and injustice through nonviolence They see a cause greater than self and are not intimidated to speak the truth. They are not willing to be a bystander when they see injustice and they are certainly not afraid to go into harms-way to get the job done that they are called to do. These are the individuals with vision, courage and confidence, yet we all reap the benefits secured by these few brave warriors who choose to travel this very arduous road.

What motivates these individuals to take such a courageous stand? They could have chosen to ignore these problematic areas of life. They could have taken a secure job and lived their lives away from inconvenience, poverty and sometimes war. Isn't a life of happiness and personal fulfillment to be sought after? For these individuals, happiness and personal fulfillment can only be secured when they are engaged in efforts to bring restoration where there is oppression and injustice. These are the individuals who put their words into action by stepping up to the plate to intercede for others as stated by Martin Luther King Jr. when he posed the question, "Life's most persistent and urgent question is, "What are you doing for others?"

The purpose of this book is to present the life of Ted Studebaker, a volunteer who provided self-help agriculture assistance in the Vietnam Central Highlands of Di Linh through Vietnam Christian Service. He was also an advocate for nonviolent peace and justice through his writing, speaking.

As Ted began his third year of service with Vietnam Christian Service, he married Pakdy, the love of his life. A few days later he was killed when forces opposing the American military launched an attack on the house where Ted lived. His story gives the reader a grasp of a common man who took a stand by living his Christian beliefs through Vietnam Christian Service. As such, his life has given cause for many to reflect on their own lives. The impact of his words and actions on his contemporaries and future generations continue to endure as a lasting force for peace.

Acknowledgments

THE CONTRIBUTIONS OF A multitude of people, made it possible to write the biography of Ted Studebaker. We thank the many individuals who responded with written information and words of encouragement for this huge endeavor, a task that took many years to culminate in this book, "Ted Studebaker, An Enduring Force for Peace."

Upon entering into this project, we soon realized that there were a vast group of Vietnam Christian Service colleagues and friends who were well acquainted with Ted and wanted us to succeed at getting his story told. In doing so, they provided us with connections in Vietnam that brought us to the very locations where Ted had lived and worked as well as friends who had lived and worked with Ted. Some of Ted's colleagues still live and work in Southeast Asia where they are providing economic development and support to people of various cultures. From these many contacts, we received written information, photographs, maps and documents. This network of support provided a wealth of assistance in our work of gathering information and telling Ted's story.

When we visited Di Linh, Vietnam, the town where Ted lived and worked, some of Ted's colleagues took us on personal guided tours of areas where Ted had lived and worked. They shared personal and endearing stories of their friendship with and admiration for Ted.

Many written accounts of Ted's life and related stories were contributed by his relatives, friends and contributing writers. All of these narratives provide a lengthy perspective into the life and persona of Ted Studebaker.

It is a pleasure to acknowledge the following individuals who provided written information, documents or photos about Ted or assisted us as we prepared for and researched Ted's life. They are: Stanley Studebaker, Zelma Studebaker, Mary Ann Cornell, Lowell Studebaker, Nancy Smith, Linda Post, Ron Studebaker, Susan Studebaker, Pakdy Studebaker, Phyllis Cribby, Julie Lutz, Jill Morris, Amy Powell, Alison Henson Bucchi, Philip Smith, Mackenzie Studebaker, Harry Peters, Verda Mae Peters, Paul Peters, Bruce Peters, Bill Herod, Howard Royer, Randy Miller, Joel Ulrich, Brad Yoder, Keith Weidner, Mr. Lai, Mr. Thu, Mr. Hai, Mr. Giau, Mr. K'Krah, Mr. K'Lai, Nguyen Trung Truc, Trinh Vinh Trinh, Tuyen Bui, Grace Mishler, Lance Woodruff, Rich Fuller, Stuart Rawlings, Fred Schmidt, Richard Tobias, Joel Freedman, Lou Pagliuca, Jean Gutshall Lindsey, Dean Hancock, Betty Vos, Donald Sensenig, Lee Brumback, Jerry Aaker, Judy Aaker, Ron Ackerman, Margaret Hancock, Wayne Keim, Marcy Ninomiya, Gayle Preheim, Earl Martin, Luke Martin, Tom Spicher, Ruth Stafford, Allen Stuckey, Jeannie Stuckey, Martha Henderson, Joy Hofacker Moore, Fonda M. Hinton Erdman, William Kostlevy, Titus Peachy, Mary Johnsen, Scott Holland, Jenny Williams, Steve Engle, Thanh Nguyen, Thong Nguyen

Acronyms

"Life's most persistent and urgent question is, 'What are you doing for others?'"
MARTIN LUTHER KING JR.

Acronym	Definition
AFSC	American Friends Service Committee
ARVN	Army of the Republic of Vietnam. This group was also referred to as the South Vietnamese Army (SVA), the official military of the Republic of South Vietnam.
BVS	Brethren Volunteer Service
CMA	Christian Missionary Alliance
CO	Conscientious objector to serving in the military
COB	Church of the Brethren
CPS	Civilian Public Service
CWS	Church World Service
DIPM	Dayton International Peace Museum
HCMC	Ho Chi Minh City (formerly Saigon)
HPI	Heifer Project International also known as Heifer International
ICSW	Institute for Clinical Social Work
IVS	International Voluntary Service
LWR	Lutheran World Relief
MACV	Military Assistance Command Vietnam. American military advisors in Vietnam

Acronym	Definition
MCC	Mennonite Central Committee
MSW	Master of Social Work
NGO	Non-Government Organization
NLF	National Liberation Front. A political organization and army in South Vietnam that fought the United States and South Vietnamese forces during the war in Vietnam (1959–1975). They had both guerrilla and regular army units, as well as a network of cadres who organized peasants in the territory it controlled.
NVA	North Vietnamese Army. North Vietnamese communists working under the same military structure as the Viet Cong.
PL	Pathet Lao, a communist nationalist group in Laos that was founded in 1950 and took control of the country in 1975. They were closely associated with North Vietnam's People's Army, South Vietnam's Viet Minh, later the Viet Cong, and Cambodia's Khmer Rouge.
PTSD	Post-Traumatic Stress Disorder. Ongoing mental and emotional stress caused by psychological trauma or injury. The person often recalls the stressful experience which interferes with health factors including sleep and relationships.
USAID	The U.S. Agency for International Development is a federal agency of the United States that provides aid to citizens of foreign countries including disaster relief, technical assistance and economic development.
UXO	Explosive weapons (bombs, shells, grenades, land mines, naval mines, cluster munition, etc.) that did not explode when they were employed and still pose a risk of detonation decades later.
VC	Viet Cong. Supporters of the communist guerrilla movement in Vietnam who fought against the South Vietnamese and the United States forces with the support of the North Vietnamese from 1954 to 1975.
VNCS or VCS	Vietnam Christian Service was a service organization of Church World Service, Lutheran World Relief and the Mennonite Central Committee. The program was formed to come to the aid of the Vietnamese who were suffering from the war. The service organization was formed in late 1965 and remained active in Vietnam until April, 1975.

Chapter 1

Not Silenced in Death

"He who is silent in the face of evil is evil."

—DIETRICH BONHOEFFER

HAVING BEGUN HIS THIRD year as an agriculture volunteer with Vietnam Christian Service and married nine days, the house where Ted, his wife, and his VNCS colleagues were living was attacked by a mortar barrage at the back door. The intruding soldiers entered the bottom level of the house from the back porch where they shot Ted to death in his bedroom shortly after midnight on April 26, 1971. As the attack began, Ted helped three VNCS workers take shelter in the closet bunker. They were Phyllis Cribby, the nurse, Daisy Banares, the rice expert, and Padky, his wife. Questions will always remain as to how and why Ted was killed. A variety of scenarios have been put forth that suggest one of the following military groups was responsible:

1. Army of the Republic of Vietnam (ARVN)

2. Viet Cong (VC)

3. North Vietnamese Army (NVA)

4. National Liberation Front (NLF)

Although the attackers could not have known Ted, the fact remains that he was an American; therefore he was considered an enemy.

Phyllis Cribby gave a very credible description of the night Ted was killed. She was in the house when she heard the gun shots that killed Ted. Below is her description:

April 27 1971
Phyllis Cribby, R.N.
Vietnam Christian Service
Di Linh

At 1:00 AM on April 26, 1971, I was still upstairs in the house. Daisy was asleep in our room downstairs and Ted and Pakdy were in their bedroom downstairs. A few minutes after 1:00 AM, a rocket mortar (the major at MACV said it was a B-40 rocket) exploded in our back yard very close to the house. This was followed by two or three more, each sounding closer and breaking some window glass. I ran downstairs and Ted was in the hall calling Pakdy. We called Daisy too (everyone had been awakened by the explosion) and all ran down the hall to the bunker. Suddenly Ted turned back and ran to his room (to check the door or get some more clothes) and just after that a charge went off by the back door. The noise and pressure from it were tremendous and we were momentarily stunned. We were afraid it might have killed Ted, but then we heard him whisper loudly, "I'm OK!" Daisy, Pakdy and I crawled quickly into the bunker. Immediately after that we heard some men enter the house. They seemed to go upstairs first and we could hear them walking around. I thought it sounded like four or five, but there may only have been two or three. Then we heard some talking in Ted's room and we heard him say khong co (not have), as if someone had asked him if we had any weapons. There was a lot of noise and confusion and I can recall hearing two volleys of shots. With the first, our dog cried out, and I thought they had killed him. We did not hear Ted say anything else. All the talking by the men was in Vietnamese, but I could not understand what they were saying. We could hear them going through our bedrooms and then someone came down the hall in our direction. I knew he would find us and probably shoot us.

I was near the door and when he opened it and shined the light in, he could only see me. I started to stand up, but he told me to get down, closed the door and walked away. We heard voices for some time more, but no one else came back to where we were. We also heard some clanking noises like they were dragging something. Pakdy thought they were taking Ted away with them. There was a little shooting outside after they left the house but none while they were still in the house. We thought ARVN soldiers might be coming, and there might be danger from them, especially if they looted the house and we saw them. We could not see what was in the hall and thought the men might have left mines or traps, so we waited for the first daylight to come out.

When I could see what was on the floor (it was just debris from the blasts), I went down the hall to Ted's room. The room was strewn with things that had been pulled from the cupboards and shelves and I went around the bed toward the closet. I saw our dog lying by the bed on that side and was surprised he was alive. He just had a wound on his front leg. The closet door was open and I could not see well into it but I thought I saw something that looked like legs near the door. I touched them and they were. I knew it was Ted. I tried to see further and although the light was still very dim I could tell he was dead. He was slumped to his right against the wall of the closet and there was a lot of blood around him and on the floor. I went to tell Pakdy and then ran over to Mr. Irwin's house next door to have him notify MACV. After the major came down, we moved Ted's body to the bed and a Catholic priest and some of our friends helped clean and dress him. His left upper arm was broken, apparently from the force of the gunshot. There were about five wounds in his chest and arm. There were no bruises on his body. A bullet shell was found on the floor near the closet. This was given to Major Wallace.

Luke Martin, author of the book, "A Vietnam Presence," wrote:

> Terry Bonnette, the Di Linh unit leader said he would likely have also been killed had he been there at the time of the attack. Both Phyllis and Terry believed strongly that it was important to continue their work in Di Linh. Terry asked: "How can a 'Christian presence' be taken seriously if we desert those who have come to trust and respect us? How can we witness to the love of God through Jesus Christ if we cannot forgive and love those who have wronged us? I feel it is important and vital enough for us to remain and even important for us to risk our lives. . . . We have decided we. . . . must take the risk. Our families in the United States understand this."

On the day of Ted's death a woman came to Pakdy and gave her $500.00 dollars. She said that the money belonged to Ted. She did not explain to Pakdy the purpose for returning the money but Pakdy suspected it may have been money borrowed from Ted or possibly some property may have been taken that was associated with Ted or VNCS.

Peace Poster

Ted had a poster hanging on his bedroom wall by the closet which stated, "SUPPOSE THEY GAVE A WAR AND NOBODY CAME." It was at this very location that Ted was killed. Even in death, his message was being expressed.

SUPPOSE THEY GAVE A WAR

...AND NOBODY CAME

"Suppose they gave a war and nobody came"

Phyllis Cribby and Pakdy accompanied Ted's body in the VNCS Land Rover driven by the local missionary, Mr. Irwin from Di Linh, to Saigon where further arrangements were made for Phyllis and Pakdy to accompany Ted's body to the Dayton, Ohio International Airport near Ted's home. This was the first time the family had meet Ted's wife Pakdy and Phyllis Cribby. The time Phyllis spent with the family was especially sustaining to all family members. She provided the family with the most factual and first-hand information about Ted's death which was a source of comfort during her week-long stay at the family farm. She and Ted had shared a mutual respect during their time in Di Linh. Their friendship remained a source of comfort to the family for the rest of their lives. It was Phyllis whom Ted had entrusted to read his letter of response to a critic a few minutes before his death. She thoughtfully made sure the letter Ted had written was copied and preserved. Phyllis provided the family with the information they needed to help them bring some closure to questions and concerns they had about the circumstances surrounding Ted's death. It was consoling for the family to learn that Father Grison, a Catholic priest administered the last rites to Ted at his death.

When the news of Ted's death had reached his parents and seven siblings, they all gathered at the home of their parents in Union, Ohio. Nearby relatives also joined the family to be supportive and simply be present. Phillip Bradley, the hometown minister was also present with the family. It was during this time that Jim Kincaid of ABC News came to the family's home to interview them for the ABC News report that was televised by Harry Reasoner the following evening (available on YouTube at Ted Studebaker ABC News Story). Local news reporters likewise came to the home of Ted's parents to interview family members in preparation for their respective news reports.

During one of the many family dialogues was a story told by Zelma, Ted's mother. She explained her observation of an unusual butterfly that appeared outside the large picture window of their home shortly after Ted's death. As she was looking out the window she noticed a butterfly fluttering as it lingered for a while. She explained how the butterfly flew closer to the window as if to be looking inside the house. It was then she noticed that the butterfly had two parallel stripes along the length of the body and a red spot at the center of its body. It was her interpretation that, "The butterfly was telling me that Ted is alright. It appeared for a brief moment, then it flew away." It was a message of consolation for the family.

Hometown Memorial Service

On Monday, May 3, 1971 the hometown memorial service was held at the Church of the Brethren in West Milton, Ohio with Rev. Phillip K. Bradley presiding. The back portion of the program contained Ted's statements of his Christian beliefs and responsibilities that accompany those beliefs. They were statements he had shared in his writings and during his speaking engagements. They were listed on the memorial service program as follows:

- "A man's life is made up of essential components such as thoughts, emotions, beliefs actions and habits. All of these components should be properly balanced and firmly set upon the solid foundation of the individual's belief in and relationship to God." TS

- "Life ultimately means taking the responsibility to find the right answers to its problems and to fulfill the tasks which it constantly sets before each individual." TS

- "I suppose we've all heard the expression: 'You've got to set some goals in life. You've got to stand for something or else you'll fall for anything.'" TS

- "My family background and my Christian upbringing in the Church of the Brethren have had a very influential effect on my choosing to become a conscientious objector." TS

- "He who takes a stand is occasionally and even often wrong, but he who never takes a stand is always wrong." TS

- "Our Father, we are thankful for the courage you give those who can dare to be different and take a stand, a stand for a true Christian witness. Make us aware of the freedom and responsibility we have as children in your kingdom. The freedom to choose and act and the responsibility to choose and act wisely." TS

- "Keep us ill at ease and restless God, as long as we can see need in the world. Help us to understand the true meaning of love and brotherhood and give us strength to say and to mean in all sincerity, 'Here am I Lord, send me.' Through Jesus Christ we pray, Amen." TS

- "Let there be a world, we pray; let there be peace on earth and let it begin with me." TS

- "For me, there is no substitute for an open-minded person searching for truth and a clearer understanding into all situations." TS

- "Can anyone ever fully understand another person until he has undergone similar experiences himself?" TS

It was from this very hometown church pulpit that Ted had presented his message, "For What It's Worth" on August 27, 1967. This was the same hometown congregation to whom he had written an open letter just months before. Among his pressing issues he had addressed with the congregation, were the following:

- "The meaninglessness, the wastefulness, and the non-necessity of this war are outweighed only by its inhumane effects, both here and in the States."

- "The killing and destruction will stop only when the American public opinion demands it."

- "I have never heard of a president pinning a medal of honor on a pacifist. These are the sacred glories reserved for those who can kill, maim, capture or destroy the most, and the more human lives involved, the more glorious the award seems to be. What a contradiction of values! How can a great society be so inconsistent and incoherent?"

The day following the church memorial service, Ted's parents, siblings and their spouses, Phyllis Cribby and Pakdy (Ted's wife) held a private memorial service at the family farm with Phillip Bradley, the local church minister presiding. The location was beside the willow tree and a nearby spring where a constant supply of cold refreshing water has never stopped flowing. It was at this spot that the family had memories of so many enjoyable activities on the farm. This was the place where the family scattered Ted's ashes in celebration of his life.

During the scattering of Ted's ashes and the days surrounding Ted's death, his father, Stanley made emotional comments about his beloved son's work for peace. Gary put Stanley's comments into the following four stanzas.

A Dad's Tears

Ted was killed in Vietnam obeying God's command.
He worked for peace nonviolently though few would understand.
Dad received the tragic news while at the old homestead.
With trembling voice he whispered,
"I hardly knew you Ted."

"Our nation will not win this war," a message Ted well knew.
Boldly did he work for peace though folks like him were few.
Dad's eyes began to water as painfully he said,
"You made us proud, in your short life.
I hardly knew you Ted."

Dad stated, "Ted is in God's hands, we'll see him now in glory."
Could it be Ted prompted us to take an inventory?
Are we living God's commands or trusting self instead?
Dad's voice then faltered as he cried,
"I hardly knew you Ted."

7

Dad spread Ted's ashes in the creek of pure life-giving water.
"Your message travels far and wide," proclaimed this grieving father.
"Isn't showing kindness the message my son spread?"
Wiping tears he tried to say,
"I hardly knew you Ted."

Saigon Memorial Service

On Friday, May 7, 1971, a memorial service was held for Ted at the International Protestant Church in Saigon. VNCS volunteers, representatives from volunteer agencies, clergy and U.S. government representatives were in attendance. Our thanks to Betty Vos, for making the memorial service program available.

MEMORIAL SERVICE
For Ted A. Studebaker
At International Protestant Church
Saigon, Vietnam
11:00 AM, Friday, May 7, 1971

Organe Prelude	
Invocation	Donald Sensenig
Congregational Song	
A Mighty Fortress Is Our God	No. 11
Scripture Reading:	Unison
1 Corinthians 13	
Lord's Prayer	Unison
Congregational Song:	#169
The King of Love My Shepherd Is	
Letter and Words of	Robert W. Miller
Remembrance	
Special Music	Lynn and Betty Vogel
Scripture Reading:	Father Tran Van Khoa
Psalm 90	
Meditations	Pastor Tran Xuan Quang
	Donald Sensenig
Closing Prayer	Pastor Doan Van Mieng
Doxology	Congregation
Postlude	

The Meditation by Donald Sensenig

I'm reminded of Abraham Lincoln's words at Gettysburg during the dedication of the Gettysburg Battlefield as a National Memorial. The circumstances are similar—we gather to reflect on the meaning of life and of death, the meaning of conflict and hatred, the meaning of "righteous causes" and how to attain them. In particular we today reflect on the life and death of our dear friend Ted Studebaker; on the conflict that has now swallowed him up along with so many, many others; on Ted's "cause" and how he worked at it.

To quote or rather paraphrase Abraham Lincoln, we have come to dedicate a place in our memory for our friend who gave his life. But in a larger sense we cannot dedicate or consecrate or hollow anything in relation to Ted. His life already has its own meaning, its own value and influence, above our poor power to add or detract. It is rather for us, the living, to be dedicated to the unfinished work, to take increased devotion to that cause for which he gave the last full measure of devotion.

What then is that unfinished work or the reason this tragedy has been brought to our attention? Each of us has our own understanding of how to use our days. We have our individual committments, some of them perhaps hidden from ourselves. We are all looking for success. We are all looking for meaning. We all want to be winners. Each of us says in his own way, "This leads to life or this leads to death." Here I believe is the heart of the matter: What is it that leads to life? On the face of things, Ted's choices led to death, perhaps an unnecessary death, a wasteful death. He could be alive now had he chosen a less exposed life, a less vulnerable place to be. But if "life" means not how long we live but how we live, maybe Ted's choice shows us something. Maybe we can leave the "how long" part up to God. Maybe the paradoxes spoken by Jesus have something to say to us this morning, something that cuts us right to the heart. "Unless a grain of wheat falls into the ground and dies, it remains alone. If you leave father and mother and wife and children for my sake, you will gain back 100 families in their place." "Blessed are the meek, for they shall inherit the earth." "Whoever tries to add onto his life will lose it. Whoever gives away his life for my sake and the sake of the Good News, he will save it."

It is not my intention to eulogize Ted Studebaker, a man who needed forgiveness like all of us, but to point out that, "he being dead, yet speaketh." Ted's life is something of a sign, pointing to the way of living that is so clearly seen in Jesus. It is a life that has implications even to that of being non-resistant to enemies. It is not a way to avoid conflict, but it tries to break the vicious cycle of violence by refusing to contribute to it. It tries to start a new kind of cycle by working at the needs that cause violence, by seeking out the have-not people and sharing of time and energy and concern, so that violence may be absorbed in constructive action. It believes that love is a stronger and more enduring power than hatred. There is no guarantee of success or even being understood. But it believes that even in failures God can be at work to bring about good.

It is a life that gives us joy to be around, a life of openness to fun and fellowship and hard work and learning, a life tuned in even to the unbeautiful people. It's a life that can be ended by a bullet or an accident, but that gives promise of sharing in the victory over death which Christ has made possible.

So this morning, let's thank God for life. Let's trust Ted in God's care, believing he is already finding new ways to learn and be useful. Let's find ways to comfort those who feel his loss most keenly. Most of all let's examine our own way of living, and dedicate ourselves to a vulnerability and unselfishness that cannot be overcome by death. That will be the most fitting memorial of all.

Survivors Guilt

Allen Stuckey, one of Ted's friends was the medical doctor who gave Ted and Pakdy their physical examinations prior to their marriage. The following experience was shared by Allen who experienced survivor's guilt upon learning of Ted's death. About ten days after Ted was killed, Allen was taken away by anti-American forces who threatened to kill him. After going through such peril his life was finally spared and he was released. However, Allen experienced survivor's guilt, knowing that Ted had been killed just days before and he was freed. Several others who knew Ted closely have shared their feelings of survivor's guilt years after his death.

Chapter 2

The Early Years

"As long as poverty, injustice and gross inequality persist in our world, none of us can truly rest."

—NELSON MANDELA

Farm where Ted was raised, Union, Ohio

It was on the family farm in Southern Ohio where Ted grew up with his parents and seven siblings. During these childhood years he developed the skills necessary to engage with others through family life, work, recreation and church participation. Born on September 29, 1945, Ted was the 7th of 8 siblings. Due to a breathing complication at birth, he required oxygen and extra time in the hospital which was critical to his survival.

Farm experiences during Ted's early childhood years contributed to his diligent work values. There was always a steady supply of responsibilities on the 144 acre farm. The family raised dairy cattle, sheep, hogs, chickens and crops of corn, wheat, oats, soybeans and hay. During his early years Ted was fascinated with the many farm encounters that included feeding the farm animals, milking the cows, observing the birth of puppies as well as calves, pigs, and sheep. He also liked to gather the chicken eggs, catch frogs in the creek and play in the barn where he and his brothers made tunnels with bales of straw. He also took an interest at working in the garden. At an early age, Ted learned to drive the tractor and helped his dad with the farm work. As a teen ager, he trapped for muskrats along the pond and creek.

Doug Studebaker (brother)

There were many notable family stories as Ted and his siblings grew up on the family farm. Ted's younger brother Doug at age four, described Ted in a letter Doug dictated while his mother wrote.

May 9, 1957

Ted and I discovered that Lady had a bunch of pups. They are about six days old. She hid them in the hay mow. Ted and I played in the hay mow. First you climb up on the bales of straw and then you crawl across the tunnel. It is best not to go in that way now because Lady might think people are trying to hurt her pups.

Ted's cow, Nettie, had a little calf. I don't help Ted milk Nettie. I just go out to the barn with him and sit down and let Ted do his own work because if I try to help him, he just sits me down. He doesn't want me to help him very much. He gets mad at me sometimes when I try to help so I always just sit down quick before he tells me to sit down and watch how he milks Nettie.

Gary and Ron's two sows both had baby pigs yesterday. One of the mother sows kept trampling on her babies. Ted and I had to keep taking the pigs away from the mother so she did not accidently kill them. Ted and I took care of them so they did not die. We kept them warm and made them comfortable. Pretty soon they began to squeal. Ted opened their mouth while I gave them milk with a spoon. Two of them died. The other ones lived.

Ted told me about the presidents. The first one was George Washington. Next was John Adams. Then there was Jefferson, Madison and Monroe. It is hard to remember more than these because Ted goes real fast and I cannot keep up with him.

I am going with Dad and Ted to put our cows in the south field where we go in our driveway because the grass is real tall out there.

Mother showed Ted and I how to make dandelion chains.

Ted and I brought Mother some lilacs and tulips that were beside the spring. Mother likes the smell of fresh flowers.

Doug

Richard Tobias (family friend)

Richard Tobias recalled an occasion when he and Ted's brother Ron, drove in the long farm lane one evening and noticed Ted was asleep in the front yard. When Ron shook him to wake him up to go to bed, they realized Ted was dreaming and he said, "Just throw me that sack of taters." Ted had helped on his uncle's potato farm which evidently accounted for the dream.

Gary Studebaker (brother)

On one occasion Ted helped me avoid a tractor breakdown. When I returned home from college, I noticed a field where the plowing was not yet finished so I hooked the plow to the John Deere tractor thinking I would help complete the job. After I had plowed the land for about ten minutes, I saw Ted walking briskly through the field toward me. He informed me, "The water has been drained out of the radiator of the tractor!" I was alarmed at my mistake and stopped plowing immediately. It was Ted's vigilance that salvaged a costly cracked engine block that day.

Ted grew to be the tallest in his family and became strong and skillful in sports. It was usually his team that was on the winning side of the many neighborhood sport competitions. He had an early start at refining his skills in athletics as the farm was well suited for building strength and endurance. It was here that he engaged with siblings and neighbors in a variety of competitive sports: softball, football, basketball, ice hockey in the winter and swimming in the summer.

During his high school years Ted earned money by doing farm work. He also maintained a job for a local plumbing company. When he obtained his driver's license he purchased a 1949 Packard. Ted prided himself in driving his car to and from school and on many occasions he enjoyed the antics of making his Packard do what few other cars could do. While driving down the road he would turn the key to the off position, hold the clutch down and turn the key back on then release the clutch (pop the clutch). The sudden mixture of gasoline with the spark in the engine produced a thunderous explosion and a startle response to any unsuspecting person within range.

Throughout Ted's elementary and secondary school years he proved to be an achiever. He easily made friends and took an interest in learning. During his high school years he participated on the football and track teams. Because of his competence in athletics he savored the competition. Ted graduated from high school in West Milton, Ohio in 1964 and continued his studies at Manchester College in Indiana in the fall of 1964.

He was a delight to his college coaches as he participated on the football and track teams. The values that Ted derived from sports participation provided enormous fulfillment. His participation on the field of athletics also provided writing topics for some of his college papers where he was able to effectively articulate the values of sports participation and their contribution to life skills.

Gary

Ted Studebaker, 1964 High School Graduation

Mary Ann Cornell (sister)

When I was 15 years old, a sophomore in high school, my brother Ted was born. It was September 1945. We lived on a 140 acre dairy farm south of West Milton and were accustomed to new babies in the family. We already had 3 girls and 3 boys, so we welcomed him and we all took care of him. I was the oldest child.

Ted was the seventh child, the first to be born in a hospital. When he was 8 years old, our brother Doug was born. My parents were farmers. My Dad and brothers did the farming, took care of the animals and the crops. My mother took care of the home and family. We learned how to work hard and long doing the chores around the farm and in the house. We never had much money but we had all we needed. We had lots of home-made fun. We listened to the radio and eventually TV programs.

We enjoyed singing around the piano while my Mom played. She taught us many songs, hymns and even harmony. Dad always sang bass. Several of my brothers including, Ted, learned to play the guitar. We had a farm pond where we swam and had picnics in the summer. We played on a raft, swung from a rope tied to a limb of a Sycamore tree and then dove into the pond. On one occasion Ted forgot to take his glasses off and they were lost in the pond. In the winter, we ice skated on the pond.

Growing up on the farm prepared us for many life experiences. My Mom was able to make a game out of work whether it was weeding our mammoth garden, shelling peas, folding diapers, milking cows or hauling manure. We learned to be flexible. Plans had to be changed because of weather, sick animals and machinery breakdowns. We had a four bedroom farmhouse with one bathroom so we learned patience, tolerance and a respect for one another and for each one's special gifts. We learned the value of work and play and the relationship of one to the other. Mom and Dad dedicated each new baby to the Lord and made a commitment to bring each child up in the knowledge of Christ. Our parents took us to church and Sunday school. We took part in youth activities and were always encouraged to go to church camp.

When Ted was in the 5th and 6th grade, he first talked of doing some volunteer work to help other people. He thought about that as part of his work in life. During his high school years he worked for a plumbing and heating contractor where he saved money for college. The war in Vietnam was being fought during his high school and college years and he became even more compelled to work for peace and understanding.

On the farm, the girls learned domestic responsibilities like sewing and cooking. The boys were often up early to milk the cows, so they wouldn't be late for school. Ted participated in FFA and 4-H projects and he took his animals to the county fair. He raised chickens, a steer and hogs. He had an exceptional interest in machinery and how to maintain it. He was only 9 years old when Dad taught him to drive the tractor with a harrow behind to cultivate the land. This caused a concerned neighbor to stop and report that a tractor was moving in the field with no one driving it.

Ted was a skillful athlete. He wrote a very meaningful essay at Manchester College after his last football game where he listed the many disciplines he had learned from his years on the football field. He was a person who didn't give up easily. He practiced hours and hours on the farm lawn until he learned to walk on his hands. Sunday afternoons he often spent time with his cousins and Doug, doing such activities as playing Monopoly while eating popcorn. When he and his friends got hungry, they would go to the kitchen and make fried egg sandwiches.

Later when Ted went to Manchester College, he was able to pay his way through college by working the night shift in the heat plant. This is where he studied for his classes as time allowed. He was persistent in his studies and was able to graduate in 3 years including summers. Immediately following graduation he prepared for graduate study at Florida State University where he had been accepted for his pursuit of a master's degree in social work. During his course of studies at Florida State University, he applied for a grant from the state government of Alabama. He was awarded the grant for which he agreed to spend two years doing social work in Alabama following the conclusion of his volunteer work in Vietnam.

Mary Ann

Ron Studebaker (brother)

Looking back in review of Ted's life, I'm fascinated by a number of facts, principles and influences that guided and supported his thinking, his decisions and his actions that eventually took him to the war-torn and far away country of Vietnam.

As I consider Ted's journey and begin to pen my thoughts, I'm confronted with several questions that may bring some sense of order to this process.

1. What is it that brought our brother Ted to his remarkable commitment to address the inhumanity he observed in the world?

2. What drove his decision to become a conscientious objector and to seek out a meaningful alternative service program in lieu of joining the military?

3. How did he prepare for and arrive at such a high level of confidence and drive in working for peace in such a troubled land?

These questions are certainly interrelated and the answers, I believe are rooted in the foundation of a caring and loving rural family life that he and all of his siblings experienced. It was a life that encouraged and fostered both a combination and balance of the following principles for living a productive and meaningful life:

- Humility with confidence
- Giving with receiving

- Listening with talking
- Hard work with hard play
- Education with responsible service
- Values and beliefs that are open minded and followed up with action

When I ponder the laser-focused life that Ted lived, I am convinced he checked off elements of all of these principles and more. However, the last principle is perhaps the most descriptive of Ted's time on this earth. Expressing his values and belief system, coupled with his open-mindedness and ready dialogue, Ted was never one to hold back from taking action on issues he knew to be right and true. This principle was exemplified many times in his detailed and somewhat confronting talk entitled "For What It's Worth" to the congregation of the West Milton Church of the Brethren in August of 1967 just prior to his departure for Vietnam.

It is important to note that Ted expressed his appreciation for the positive role the church had on his decision to embrace conscientious objection in serving both his God and country. He stated, "I love the church for helping to shape me into the kind of person I want to be."

While nearly eight years older than Ted, I do recall his love for just being outdoors, playing with the dog, helping feed the animals, gathering eggs, playing ice hockey, softball and touch football with his siblings and cousins. He cherished the farm life and acquired a sacred appreciation for God's natural order, especially the relationship of man to the plant and animal kingdoms. Thus, his affinity for all things connected to agriculture.

During my research and review process for this writing assignment, I took the opportunity to reread a paper that Ted had written for a philosophy class at Manchester. It describes in some detail, the extent of his thought process and values as he arrived at his decision to register as a conscientious objector.

Reviewing his paper refreshed my memory of my own journey at taking the position of conscientious objection beginning in the mid 1950's. Ted had obviously over-heard some intense discussion I was having with Mom regarding my thoughts and decision process on this topic and Brethren Volunteer Service. Ted, eight or nine years old at the time, came to me one evening with a very serious question; "Ronnie, what is a conscious rejector?" After some laughs, we engaged in a serious and rather detailed discussion explaining conscientious objection, pacifism, and military service. He was, of course aware of Lowell having served in the

Army. I recall Ted's serious questions about how and why one goes to the military, and for how long.

Likewise, he posed some very interesting queries about alternative service, i.e.: "Where do you go?" "Do you get paid?" "Can you come home if you don't like it?" "Why do some people need help?" I do recall both Mom and Dad being very fascinated by his inquisitiveness at that time and age.

Certainly Ted was nurtured by loving, Christian parents and influenced by the teaching and values learned at the church. As well, he was influenced by the experiences, endeavors and examples of his siblings, notwithstanding the differing range in ages.

For much of Ted's teen years, I was gone from home, either in college or in Morocco as a part of my alternative service. However, Mom was so very good about keeping us informed of the happenings on the farm and the "comings and goings" of her flock.

From all accounts while yet in high school, Ted had become a strong and independent thinker who readily assumed responsible leadership among his peers. This was evident in his classroom assignments and activities, his many agricultural projects and his all-out commitment to athletic competition in football, track and wrestling.

Ted was so aptly described at that time by Keith Weidner, his high school English teacher; "A cheerful, smiling, vibrantly alive boy in my classroom among others very much like him; a red-jerseyed competitor, a fierce and jarring tackler on the gridiron; a willing and unstinting giver of himself in class projects; a good humored and uninhibited performer. . . . "

As he registered with the local Selective Service Board at his 18th birthday, Ted was very clear and firm in his rationale and decision to serve as a conscientious objector. He had also expressed his appreciation to his country and government for offering that freedom of choice. "I feel and know that I can live up to my beliefs and better this world more as a C.O. in an alternative service than as a soldier in the U.S. Army."

When Ted entered Manchester College, it was clear to all who knew him that he was there to fully participate, absorb and benefit in any and every way possible. In addition to an overload of academic classes, he played football, regularly carried out deputation services to area churches, participated in Bible study and taught Sunday school classes, all this while working a scheduled job in the campus power plant.

Ted's selection of classes, professors, friends and campus activities certainly provided him ample opportunity to share and enrich his beliefs and values as a conscientious objector. Others who influenced his thinking and actions regarding pacifism were Jesus, Mahatma Gandhi, Albert Schweitzer, and Dietrich Bonhoeffer.

Ted's total immersion into Manchester's broad liberal arts education was an excellent fit. His thought process, his open inquiring mind and his endless tenacity are what set him apart and likewise moved him forward. He possessed a unique ability to force and challenge the dialogue and discussions, pose questions, craft solutions and answers for himself. This was for Ted a very logical and straightforward process that brought results. He loved the challenge of reasonable discussion and differing views; as this allowed him to sort out and firm up his own convictions, values and approach to the real world.

Ted pointed out in his message to the home church, the tremendous value he received from his intense "give and take" sessions with fellow students and professors. One of the many late night discussions that carried a lasting impact on Ted's thinking centered on the Book of James which emphasizes the value of faith that is based on action. Not simply talking the talk, but actually walking the walk. In my view, this concept of action was perhaps "the" major concept underlying Ted's decision and commitment to eventually put his beliefs and values to work. As he clearly stated in his letter to the West Milton Church, "Here I stand, God helping me, I can do no other."

Upon graduating from Manchester College, Ted traveled to Tallahassee as he had been accepted into Florida State University's Graduate School of Social Work. This intense two-year program broadened Ted's preparation for his future work, especially in the areas of inter-agency cooperation, coordination and delivery of services, as well as methods and techniques to foster self-help and independence. Ted's amazing thirst for truth and knowledge is what fueled his seemingly insatiable appetite as he prepared himself for the road ahead. He exhibited such urgency on this educational journey that in retrospect one could almost assume he already knew his time was limited.

Following his orientation training with Brethren Volunteer Service, Ted was then assigned to Vietnam Christian Service as an agriculture specialist. It was there in the Central Highlands area of Di Linh, Vietnam that Ted was able to apply the principles, values and skills of the peacemaker he had become.

He went to a troubled land to share of himself, to be a friend and to help in any way he could. His willingness to acquire the languages, share his music, and utilize his agricultural expertise, readily made him a welcome and integral part of that community for over two years.

In April 1971, Ted's life was ended by Vietcong soldiers who had entered the Vietnam Christian Service house. Ted's life was brief but productive. The story of his unselfish journey has had a positive impact whenever it is shared.

Subsequent to Ted's passing, some individuals have suggested that he may have been naive about the realities of the war in Vietnam in relation to his own daily activities. Others have asked if Ted was truly aware of the dangers he faced in such a chaotic and troubled land.

Ted was clearly troubled by what he viewed as the immorality, the injustice and the mindless destruction of life and property in Vietnam. This was the inhumanity he saw and felt. It fueled his daily work. Certainly he was aware of the danger around him. It was a war zone. He and his team were indeed cognizant of their situation and routinely took necessary precautions in an attempt to remain safe.

Simply stated, Ted chose the high road led by his conscience, to freely give of his love and talents to his neighbors in a war-torn land. He was fully prepared and armed with confidence in the mission that God had set before him. He was totally committed to giving of himself without reservation.

Ted the peacemaker, truly followed the words of the Prophet Micah whom he quoted to his hometown congregation, "What does the Lord require of you, but to do justice, love kindness and walk humbly with your God."

Ted Studebaker's life of faith spoke volumes through his actions. Accordingly he truly gave his all!

Ron

In 1956 at the age of 10 Ted attended a community event to hear a sermon by Reverend Bob Richards, the world champion pole vaulter at that time and a Church of the Brethren minister. Bob preached a series of sermons at the local high school. It was during the alter call at one of these services that Ted publically walked forward and dedicated his life to Christ. He communicated his Christian values through his participation on the deputation team during his Manchester College years and in subsequent papers. While serving in Vietnam, Ted continued to express his Christian values with confidence in his diary entries.

Ted and his brother Gary were students at Manchester College at the same time for one term when Gary returned to the college for an independent study. On weekends, Gary visited with Ted and his roommates at the house where they were staying. One of his roommates was a Muslim from Turkey. It was during their sharing that Gary observed Ted's maturity and inclusive personality as he communicated with all of his roommates with calmness and ease. Ted could disagree without being disagreeable. His maturity at sharing, listening and responding, contributed to the respect and friendship that was so apparent to Gary during these weekend visits.

Volunteer service was a way of life in Ted's childhood environment. He was aware that his mother sent relief packages to war victims in Germany. He was also aware of his dad's volunteer work for Heifer Project when his dad assisted in transporting cattle from Texas to families in Mexico. Ted observed as his brother Ron worked through Brethren Volunteer Service in construction projects in Agadir, Morocco after a devastating earthquake in 1960. Another brother, Gary worked through International Voluntary Service in Laos in the mid-1960s doing agriculture work. Accordingly, the idea of volunteer service was a part of Ted's mindset from his earliest years. Eventually he experienced all of his siblings doing volunteer work at some point in their respective lives.

Being the seventh of eight children, Ted noted that his siblings were pursuing careers in the social service areas. At a young age he seemed to have a grasp of the concept that people need help at dealing with poverty, personal challenges, natural disasters and war. As such, he recognized the value of volunteer work and the need to advocate and offer services. Therefore, his mindset from the beginning was to prepare himself for a life of service.

Chapter 3

The College Years

"We can't talk about the poor. We must be poor with the poor.
Then there is no doubt how to act."

—SISTER DOROTHY STANG

AFTER COMPLETING HIGH SCHOOL Ted entered Manchester College in the fall of 1964 where he came with some goals in mind. He wanted to prepare himself for work in the area of social relations, participate in college athletics and to work his way through college as much as possible. He majored in sociology and psychology. His decision to work for peace and justice would be shaped in some of his classes by a few professors and many discussions. He had brought with him to Manchester College, a determination to make wise use of his years. Accordingly, he found a sufficient number of classes taught by professors who were thought provoking and stimulating especially in the social areas where he was inquisitive and thrived in the dialogue.

One of Ted's good friends and a roommate at Manchester College was Fred Schmidt. Fred vividly recalled some of the noteworthy times he and Ted had during their college years.

Ted and I were first acquainted when I came to Manchester as a freshman football player. We made contact (literally) on the practice field. It was not long until we both learned that we shared the same state and some common interests. We also soon became somewhat of a foursome as we ran around together with Ned Harms and Larry Buck. We became Ned/Ted/Fred and Buck. Over the next few years Ted and I became roommates along with

23

various others joining us at the Shull house and we worked together at various jobs around Manchester, including the Farm Bureau
Co-op and mostly at the heat plant on campus where we often
competed to see who could work the longest shift. I'm not sure
who won out but each of us worked 3 to 4 days at 24 hour per day
shifts over the breaks when the other one went home for a day or
two, which neither of us did very often. Paul Shrider, our boss was
not real happy when he found out how many hours we had worked
because we have to "sleep on the job" sometimes.

I do recall that Ted and I competed in a friendly way in many
things, most of which were physical and which Ted often prevailed.
However, in one instance I started to practice on the speed bag in
the Goshorn building (which we called the gosh darn building)
when I was working at the heat plant and Ted did not know I was
learning some skills on the speed bag. Then one day some weeks
later we were in the weight room lifting weights. He went over to
the speed bag for a bit and I asked if he could teach me how to do
it. He said "ok" and at first I stumbled around and then went on a
terror and his eyes went wide and he said, "Dad burn it roommate
you've been practicing." We both had a good laugh and I just said,
"You must just be a good teacher."

These were the times we had adventures with the girls, trips to
the golf course stadium at night for some "free sodas," learning to
play the guitar, setting a school record for a 4 man bike team at the
May Day race around the then cinder track and going on deputation teams with his cousin John whom we called #2.

The deputation trips were one way we explored our faith.
Through the college church relations office the deputation team
offered to help local churches with any part of their service either
as worship leaders or speakers. Ted's cousin, John Studebaker participated in the deputation team presentations and he also sang.

In one particular service Ted and I presented a dialog between
one person who was a conscientious objector and one who challenged that position. The challenger offered a hypothetical situation about a grandmother driving a car and what would the CO
do if . . . ? With each answer the challenger changed the situation
to put the CO in a no win scenario. This drama usually opened up
a good dialog following the service.

One of the most memorable things Ted and I shared was his
learning to play the guitar. He of course went on to be a pretty
good player. These were the days of hootenanny and folk song
glory. Ted worked with me on some guitar chords and I began to
learn some simple songs.

On another occasion I injured my knee as I trained for throwing the javelin for the track team. I was in the Wabash hospital to have it operated on. I was in a cast and on crutches for over 6 weeks and could not compete with the team that year. The only hospital visitors I got other than my own dad were Claude Wolfe, and yes you guessed it, Ted. He rode one of the competition bikes from Manchester to Wabash, a distance of 17 miles to visit me as part of a training regimen for the race. What a feat, but you know Ted and he gutted it out.

When Ted and I lived in Shull house (at Manchester College), Bill Kilgore joined us as a roommate as did John Studebaker. This presented a dilemma since I called Ted only by his last name and now there were two Studebakers. So we started calling Ted, Studebaker #1 and John Studebaker #2 which soon changed to 1 and 2. I became #3 and Bill Kilgore became #4.

Girls! This was a particularly sensitive topic for Ted. John was still connected with his then Puerto Rican love whom he met while in alternative service and Bill was beginning to see his future wife Ev Mason. I was beginning to connect with Mary Shearer who later became my first wife. At this time Ted did not yet have a girlfriend, though we finally did work on him enough that he went on a date with Bev Sayers. Our girlfriends then became 1.1 or 2.1 or 3.1 etc. But Ted did not stay with his. We really did not have much luck at getting him "hooked up" again, in fact, while he was in graduate school in Florida, he did meet someone, but nothing serious until he met and married Pakdy.

Fred

On one occasion Ted's dad, Stanley flew his airplane to Manchester College to visit with Ted. After the visit, Ted was working in the heat plant where he wrote a letter to his dad to share his feelings and appreciation for him:

May 26, 1965, 10:00 pm

Dad,

Hope you had a good flight home. The guys here were surely glad to be able to fly for the first time and especially Mrs. Shull.

Thanks for the $125 shekels. That should be all I need to get through summer school.

I felt a little disturbed about not being able to have a good honest talk with you while you were up here. If college has taught me anything, it has taught me to be honest in my relationships, cause if I'm not honest, I'll just become another "phony" person striving to satisfy my own whims and selfish wishes. In other words, if I ever expect to establish a true friendship relation with anyone, I'm going to have to express my feelings and values overtly and not hide what I feel to be right. I like to think of myself as a thinking individual; independent and free to act and say what I have learned to be "right." Sometimes this means breaking away from the traditional ties to become your "real self" at your honest best. Well I've got a long way to go Dad, because sometimes it's very difficult for me to "think well" and to be "honest" and humble. Do you understand what I mean? I remember some words I read once by Pascal: "Let us strive then to think well, for herein lies the principal of morality."

Guess I sound like some way out philosopher ugh? At any rate, what I've said holds great meaning for me and I thought you might profit from it, argue it, disagree, or whatever.

I wish you a real good experience and a safe flight on your trip.

Sincerely,

Ted

The following closing prayer was presented by Ted at a deputation team service:

Our Father as we come before you at this special day of worship, keep us always aware of the many blessings which are ours daily. As we pause just now to reflect a bit, we think of many troubled people and places in the world. People who are hungry, without shelter and heavily burdened people who know you not. Grant us the wisdom to at least understand their problems and instill within us a desire to want to help them. We can think of war torn countries in Southeast Asia and other parts of the world where death and destruction are ever present. We pray that man may realize his responsibility and duty to his fellowman, to cease this dehumanization process and study war no more, so that man may live in peace on earth.

Help us to be truthful and honest with ourselves and with others in all our relationships. Take away our self-centeredness which comes with confusion and the luxury in which we live. Open our hearts and minds to your ways and to the example set before us by your Son's mission on earth.

Make us aware of the freedom and responsibility we have as children in your kingdom, the freedom to choose and act and the responsibility to choose and act wisely. Help us to realize that as Christians, the ultimate truth, the ultimate meaning in our lives, lies in our relationship with you, God. Give us the courage to turn to you in our daily routines, in our work and in our relationships with others. We need you in the center of life. For our daily life is our temple and our religion.

Keep us ill at ease and restless, God, as long as we can see needs in the world. Help us to understand the true meaning of love and brotherhood and open up our hearts to the rewards and joys of service.

We pray that you would give us strength to say and to mean in all sincerity: "Here am I Lord, send me."

You know the desires and needs of each of us, God. Perhaps in silence you will have something to say to us if we listen.

As Ted planned for his college studies he was especially interested in social, moral and ethical issues. This was evident in the books he read and the papers he wrote. He was especially intrigued by two Christian authors, Dietrich Bonhoeffer and Thomas Kempis. The Bible prompted his thinking and he often wrote his thoughts in the margins of these books supporting, opposing or elaborating his own views as he read.

Dietrich Bonhoeffer, a German Lutheran pastor was assassinated at the age of 39 by Adolph Hitler for his open defiance of Hitler's ruthless strategies. Although Ted did not always agree with all of Bonhoeffer's opinions, he developed a high respect for this man's moral positions. Ted selected the following five statements by Bonhoeffer, to review and support or oppose in a class at Manchester College.

1. "We must learn to regard people less in the light of what they do or omit to do, and more in light of what they suffer."

2. "I discovered later in life and I'm still discovering right up to this moment that it is only by living completely in this world that one learns to have faith. By this worldliness I mean living unreservedly in life's duties, problems, successes and failures. In doing so we throw ourselves completely into the arms of God taking seriously not our own sufferings, but those of God in the world. That, I think, is faith."

3. "When Christ calls a man, he bids him come and die."

4. "Being a Christian is less about cautiously avoiding sin than about courageously and actively doing God's will."

5. "The fearful danger of the present time that is above the cry for authority, we forget that man stands alone before the ultimate authority and that anyone who lays violent hands on man here is infringing on eternal laws and taking upon himself superhuman authority which will eventually crush him."

One of Ted's assigned readings at Manchester College was the book entitled "Imitation of Christ" by Thomas Kempis, a book that is based on the life of Christ. Kempis, a student of the Bible was a German priest and a writer of Biblical commentary in the early 1400s. Ted's commentary throughout the book indicates his high interest in the writings of Kempis. Below are a few of Ted's own written comments that he regarded as truths presented in this thought provoking book:

1. "We are called to imitate the life of Christ."

2. "We are called to serve Christ."

3. "All is vanity except to love and serve God only."

4. "Vanity is to follow the desires of the flesh."

5. "Acknowledge your own ignorance."

6. "Love to be unknown and esteemed not."

Although Ted noted that some statements by Kempis were impractical to support, he selected the following statements which he could support. He presented and defended these in a presentation in one of his classes.

1. "Keep thyself as a stranger and pilgrim upon this earth and as one to whom the affairs of this world do not appertain."

2. "Unto the humble He revealeth His secrets and sweetly draweth and invitith him unto Himself."

3. "Without a friend thou canst not live well; and if Jesus be not above all a friend to thee, thou shall be indeed sad and desolate."

4. "Jesus hath now many lovers of His heavenly kingdom, but few bearers of His Cross."

5. "The true profiting of a man is the denying of himself; and a man that hath denied himself is exceedingly free and secure."

6. "The sufferings of this present time are not worthy to be compared with the future glory that shall be revealed in us."

Being aware of various positions and points of view, Ted prepared himself to defend his personal beliefs. Accordingly he engaged with people, read subjects of interest, listened and considered the consequences of his actions. He was candid at expressing his views but also prepared with thoughtful questions. In doing so he demanded of himself the need to live up to responsible personal standards.

His journal entries reflected a desire to wisely use time, money and resources. This was evident with his material possessions and his work ethic. He considered the world condition and realized the need for compassion. Accordingly, he made choices that would prepare him to address these troubling conditions. With such a mindset, there was no need for personal gain or for things that would lead to an easy road in life. This is not to say he was not without misgivings and failures in life. There was also a maturity in dealing with those who rejected him. Even though he candidly, self-criticized in his writings, he continued the pursuit of ways to use his failures as a stepping stone to learning, to engage and to make contributions. Several of his diary statements revealed an honesty and openness about his need to be self-disciplined in order to be accountable.

In some of his lighter moments there was a mixture of wit, humor and sometimes self-deprecation. It was an easy going, quiet persona which came across in his relationships, yet on the serious side, he articulated his thoughts with confidence and candor as noted in the many papers he wrote. Those who heard him speak were aware of his articulate presentation. When it came to the important issues in life he was well read and sometimes quoted examples from the life of Christ, biblical scripture, voices with historical experience and even examples from his own experiences.

Upon approaching his 18th birthday Ted had been giving careful thought to the rational for his position as a conscientious objector. Accordingly he was prepared for his response to the draft board. A few years later he wrote a paper for his philosophy class at Manchester College where he expressed his beliefs as a conscientious objector. In his paper (below), he explained how he arrived at this momentous decision.

My Rights and Values as a C.O.

At the coming of my 18th birthday, I like every 18 year old boy must register at my local draft office and declare my personal beliefs in the area of militarism and war. For most boys, I suppose over 90 percent, it would not be difficult just to fill out the information in the normal expected manner saying that they would go to the army if called and they would go to war, fight and kill if necessary for their country. But what about the boys who couldn't conscientiously agree to the latter requirements? Are these conscientious objectors who call themselves pacifists any less patriotic and devoted or do they just find their beliefs and values different? Speaking for myself, since I am a C.O., I don't feel unpatriotic or disloyal to my country. However, I do think there are certain rights, beliefs, and values to which one should be more devoted than his country if he has arrived at them through conscientious thought, learning and experience. I simply would like to live my life in a manner that I have learned and believe to be right. I feel and know that I can live up to my beliefs and better this world more as a C.O. in an alternative service than as a soldier in the U.S. army. I value my right to be a C.O. very highly for I realize that not every country offers her boys a choice.

I think that by saying that I value my right to choose to be a C.O., I am also admitting that I value, the government and country that offered this freedom of choice to me. In this way I am patriotic and loyal. The values which I can find by going into alternative service as a C.O. rather than the Army seem to be more rewarding to me in all ways except of course, pay. But if I truly value and take seriously my pacifistic stand, I won't mind taking ten dollars a month for a salary because I'm standing up for my convictions and that's what really counts.

I believe that values are a personal thing which must be developed and exercised by the individual. It would be of no value to me if my C.O. convictions were forced upon me against my will or if I became a C.O. just to be a draft-dodger. Values can only have meaning if they're established through beliefs that have been thought out and accepted as true and right in the mind of the individual.

It seems to me that freedom is the foremost of all values especially the freedom to choose what we believe. In choosing to be a C.O., I was only exercising my right to freedom of choice which I value as the most important freedom. For me war, force and killing are certainly no way to improve the situation in the world. If I can't give at least two years of my life in an alternative service, to the loving and peaceful betterment of this world and mankind, then I am not living up to my sacred values and convictions.

When talking of conscientious objection and pacifism, my thoughts automatically turn to one of the greatest pacifists of all time, Gandhi.

Although I don't agree with all that he said and did, I have tremendous respect for the beliefs and values which he stood for and upheld. Perhaps the words to this verse of a folk song which speaks of Gandhi can best relate my values and feelings as a C.O. and pacifist.

> "Gandhi spoke of freedom one night,
> They said, man you've gotta fight.
> He said yes, but love's the weapon we must use.
> For with killing no one wins,
> It's with love that peace begins,
> We're all brothers and we're only passin' thru."

Ted had an appreciation for the nonviolent peace movement pioneers who sacrificed their time and energy to enable him and others like him to serve through nonviolent peace making programs without being forced to violate their beliefs. Some of these pioneers were persecuted, imprisoned and even put to death for their conscientious objection beliefs, yet their contributions to peace through nonviolence was realized through the years by the accumulation of many nonviolent peace landmarks.

Date	Timeline of Selected Nonviolent Peace Landmarks
1492–1763	Resistance to compulsory military service for religious or ethical reasons existed for a small number of citizens during the colonial period.
1525–1708	The historic peace churches were founded: Mennonites (1525), Society of Friends (1624), Amish (1644) and Church of the Brethren (1708).
1815	The first peace organizations for conscientious objectors were established in some of the eastern coastal states. Since then more peace organizations have developed.
1861–1865	There were no provisions for conscientious objection during the Civil War on both sides. They sometimes endured violent persecution and even death by a firing squad. For the first time government officials debated conscientious objection at the national level. They eventually offered the option of noncombatant service which remained in effect through World War I.
1917	The American Friends Service Committee (AFSC) was founded to provide young Quakers and other conscientious objectors to war, with an opportunity to perform alternative service during wartime.
1917	The Selective Service Act of 1917 provided for conscientious objectors but they were required to serve in noncombatant military positions. Those who rejected any form of military association were sentenced to harsh treatment in federal military prisons where some died.

Date	Timeline of Selected Nonviolent Peace Landmarks
1935	Representatives from the historic peace churches (Brethren, Mennonite and Friends) prepared their positions on conscientious objection and alternative service for presentation to President Franklin Roosevelt who was not sympathetic.
1940	The Selective Service Training Act passed creating noncombatant service in the military. These individuals were assigned to perform work of national importance under civilian direction.
1941	The Civilian Public Service Program was implemented. Conscientious objectors were assigned to alternative service at camps where they worked in soil conservation, forestry, farming, care for the mentally ill and work as test subjects for medical experiments. All work was performed without pay.
1948	Brethren Voluntary Service was founded. BVS provides an alternative to military service for conscientious objectors. Volunteers work in a wide range of projects serving needs locally and around the world.
1948	Gladys Muir, peace studies professor and member of the Church of the Brethren established the nation's first peace studies program in the United States at Manchester College. Many colleges have followed.
1965	The World Friendship Center was Founded in Hiroshima, Japan. The center promotes peace through classroom instruction, Peace Park tours and stories from survivors of the atomic bomb. A variety of community based peace activities are presented to educate the public about the inhuman consequences of nuclear war.
1965	Vietnam Christian Service was formed in 1965 and remained active in Vietnam until April, 1975. Volunteers provided their expertise and assistance in self-help projects of agriculture, construction, health care, education and economic development.
1975	The Peace Resource Center was founded at Wilmington College by the Quaker peace activist Barbara Reynolds. The center provides students with practicums and internships in nonviolence, social justice and global peace. The center also houses "The Barbara Reynolds Papers" (the Hiroshima and Nagasaki Memorial Collection).
1987	The Lion and Lamb Peace Arts Center was established at Bluffton College. Visitors learn about peace, justice, cultural understanding and nonviolent responses to conflict by interacting with literature and the arts. The center provides resources for students, teachers, parents, and the community.
2001	The Gladys Muir Peace Garden was established at Manchester College for visitors to learn about peace and justice. Peace heroes are recognized with plaques on the Peace Wall and in the peace garden. The house adjacent to the garden provides a place for classes to discuss peace issues.

Date	Timeline of Selected Nonviolent Peace Landmarks
2004	The Dayton International Peace Museum was founded to raise awareness of nonviolent strategies for achieving peace. Visitors learn about peace, justice and nonviolence. They also celebrate the lives of peace heroes whose stories are on display.

The Heat Plant

The heat plant at Manchester College is where Ted worked to pay his way through college. Ted was one of three college students who operated the heat plant during his Manchester College years. This employment opportunity came about because he had a related experience when he had worked for a plumbing and heating company during the summer months of his high school years. His earlier preparation proved to be the right fit for his skills. The job called for monitoring the thermostats and shoveling coal into the giant furnaces to provide heat to the many buildings on the college campus. Ted maintained this job for 6 hours per day, every weekday from 12:30 pm to 2:30 pm and again from 6:00 pm to 10:00 pm when he shut the system down. On weekends, he worked 15 hours for a total of 45 hours per week. He kept this job until he graduated three years later. During those three years Ted took an average of 17 units of college courses per term for four quarter terms per year. He was also a member of the varsity football and track teams for three years and he participated on the wrestling team for one season. Accordingly, he planned his schedule carefully so he could attend his college classes, study, participate with his teammates in sports, participate in the college deputation team and get his sleep. He did most of his studies in the heat plant. He realized that such a study plan had the advantages of being away from the distractions that would probably occur elsewhere on campus. Through it all he was able to maintain good grades and complete his college objectives. But with such a demanding schedule there were times when he would doze off on the job for a few minutes. On one occasion Ted took what he intended to be a brief nap. Much later when the night watchman was making his rounds, he found Ted sound asleep and had to wake him up. It was then Ted realized he had been sleeping on the job for about three hours and the thermostats were lower than they should have been. He immediately shoveled the necessary coal into the furnace to correct the deficiency. Ted and the night watchman became good friends but Ted especially appreciated this wake-up call.

The night watchman owned a 140-acre farm a few miles from the campus where he invited Ted to ride horses. Ted related well to horses and horseback riding during the several times he went to his friend's farm to ride horses. He had become quite skillful at handling horses. On one occasion Ted rode one of the horses in a college parade. At another time when Ted was free, he took Gary with him to the horse farm where they both rode the horses. That is until Gary's horse realized that Gary was not a horseman and bolted for the narrow barn door opening at a high speed. Ted had the satisfaction of seeing Gary jump off the horse in the nick of time, before the horse ran through the barn door that was wide enough for the horse only.

During Ted's second year at Manchester College, his brother Gary visited him in the heat plant as Ted worked the night shift. Both brothers sat at the table and talked into the night in the isolated furnace room below ground level where the only sound was the muffled roar of the furnace fires producing heat for the campus buildings. Gary realized how this would be the ideal place to study without the usual interruptions of campus life. At one point, Gary volunteered and Ted allowed him to shovel coal and clear the ashes from the huge furnaces. At about midnight, Gary began to get tired and reluctantly said "Good-bye" as he left. He was hesitant to leave as he realized Ted had a few more hours on the job as well as many other ongoing responsibilities as a college student. As Gary departed, he began to grasp the enormous discipline, planning and maturity it took for Ted to maintain his college schedule which included many responsibilities beyond the 45 hours per week in the heat plant. He thought about Ted's participation in the Saturday football games which included football practice in the fall, deputation team preparation with the Sunday morning presentations, attending five classes per term, eating and sleeping. Gary left the heat plant that night with an intense feeling of respect for Ted's diligence and work, but even more salient was his calm persona and ease of acceptance of those in his environment. It was a thought provoking night that Gary recalls with profound admiration for these rare qualities that we are all attracted to.

During Ted's time on this job, the heat plant occasionally became a place for social gatherings. His peers, football buddies and even coeds came down the steps to the heat plant to talk with Ted and he appreciated the gatherings. One evening after his final college football game he began thinking about the many values and lessons the team sport of football had provided for him so he began to articulate his thoughts on paper. He real-ized that he was caught up with the work of shoveling coal and monitoring gauges for a while so he began to write. He also made a notation on the side of his paper, "Since this is not a required assignment, no one will read this paper anyway." The following is the paper that Ted wrote.

Why I Play Football

Now is your big chance Stud. You've got all the ashes out and one hour left to put into words, your most prized and sacred thoughts, next to God himself of course.

Why did I ever play football? Oh darn, how should I begin? Why of course, just be honest boy; after all, this is only a letter to yourself, not to Mr. Leffel at the downtown paper.

I played football for "glory." Yea boy, all the glory I could get, that's why I put on the pads for mostly, I think. And don't think it didn't bring glory. Ask anybody on campus, they'll all tell you how wonderful it must be to be on the team. It's status, prestige and an ego builder, now man, ain't that glory? Now that I think on it, there's a heck of a lot of reasons why I played football. Some are positive, some are negative, but with God's help they're all honest. I played football because I was forced to. Not quite liter-ally of course. I naturally do as my big brothers do, so if the big Studs, Lowell, Ron and Gary play the game, then so does this Stud. It's just tradition at our house. Also, it was just the thing to do at good ole M.U. High School. Kid, you're not with it if you don't get out there and crack. I figure people can force you physically, and people can force you mentally, but the greatest of these is mentally. I played football because I gotta show people I'm a man, or at least a pretty strong boy. You can't be a weakling like Alan Elifritz and play this sport, unless of course you go out for QB. When a boy gets through with two weeks of summer practice, I'll give him the title of man without any questions asked, he deserves it.

I played football because it's fun, sometimes, but usually it's not fun at all. I guess it's only mostly fun when you're raking in glory. It just ain't fun to work under the smiling sun in late August till you start imagining cool springs and cold lemonade, or maybe you wish you could faint or just get hurt or just plain die. Anything but continue the dehumanizing experience of football practice. Personally I spent quite a few of my hours of football practice in hell and that ain't fun. That is unless, of course you look back on it later and call it suffering, then it's OK.

I played football because it takes what 90% of the kids I know ain't got. Coaches call this quality various names; intestinal fortitude, desire; ability; I'd rather just call it "guts." It's got that masculine connotation, don't you agree? I just thought, I got it and they don't, or do they and they'd rather use it on something else. Anyway I'm in the elite 10% when it comes to playing football and that makes me a hero of sorts by most standards. I played football because if I'm good enough, I'll get enough quarters in to get that long sought after letter. Judas Priest, the work and sweat and mental strain I poured out for that measly letter award could buy a new car if work, sweat and mental strain like that were transferable into money.

**Half time at the Manchester, Earlham football game.
Ted's senior year.**

I played football so I could act out some kind of an athletic expert and shoot the bull with all the guys when those all important social conversations commence. Now there's some real satisfaction if you've got the right names and statistics in your head at the right time.

I played football because Mom would let me and Dad thought it was foolish. Anyway, Mom rules in our house. Besides, I'd rather be gaining glory on the gridiron than slopping shoats or shoveling manure.

I played football because, dad burn, I just can't deny it anymore, because I want the girls to notice. I often daydreamed about pulling in some fantabulous interception or making some earth shaking tackle that would win the game for us so all the nice looking girls, sometimes special ones, would notice and then I'd have to "fight em off." Or I wished I could have a flying tackle to knock a ball carrier out of bounds and in the process I happened to knock down a few cheerleaders. Why I'd pick em up and say "Excuse me," and then run back to the huddle while they stared in awe. How asinine! How stupid to think those thoughts! It never would happen in a million years.

I played football because I hate it. But you see, I like to suffer for righteousness and self-discipline, it's what keeps me going. So even if I hate it, I love it, because to suffer, for righteousness is next to Godliness and that sounds good to me. I've learned a lot about self-discipline through football, and that came through suffering. Thus, I say I hate it, but really I love it, see?

I played football because I always wanted to get injured and I got my share all right. But I was kind of disappointed because getting injured didn't bring me all the glory I thought it would. I don't know that I ever broke a bone, but I can think of about $ 200 worth of doctor bills that football insurance had to shell out for me. They even bought me a $ 5.00 jock for my mal-formed vertebras. That's what I call real support. Oh yes, I gave the ice packs, the tape, the cramergesic, the Atomic Balm and the whirl pool pretty good use too. Heck, I might be sterile by now for all I know. They tell me if you stay in the whirl pool too much it tends to put the quietus on ya like that.

I played football to travel. It's nice to get to ride the bus with the big boys and see all the other campuses, stay overnight in motels, eat in good restaurants and wear my flashy sport coat.

I played football because if I ever met a true friend, chances are he's gonna have to have played football first. Look at Duck, Kyser, Harms, even ole Schmitzy.

I played football because I want to hurt people, and I've done it too. I've put men out of the game, but I've also been put out myself. You can't call a brotherly love conference when they're running a power sweep on your end with a guard and a halfback leading. So I try to hurt.

I've got ten minutes to close. I could probably write all night before I would exhaust all the reasons why I played football. Dad burn, I blocked and tackled, I hit and cracked, I sweat and hurt, I won and lost, I cried and I laughed football for nine years under an organized team. I swear right here before God and myself that it was the greatest experience I have ever had. I memorized those four signs and I do believe that the best way out of trouble is through it, and that there is no greater immorality than to occupy a place you cannot fill, and that if I fear God I need not fear any man. I was a Bulldog and I was a Spartan. I was a guard and I was a linebacker. I put on the pads and I used em. I kept my body in shape and it hurt but it was worth it. I won and I lost, I found personal glory and success and I found ridicule and failure. I lost contacts, but I spent money and kept em replaced. I did the best job I knew how, I got my rewards and only I know what they are.

Now it's all over. I'll never put on the pads again. But nobody will ever take those thoughts of why I played football away from me. I prayed to God to let me play and he did. Now I can finish my life with a feeling of intense personal pride, a sense of great accomplishment, sensitivity and humbleness toward others and a whole heck of a lot of self-discipline and it's all because I once played a game called football.

Written in January 1967 after my last football season, from the heat plant.

Ted Studebaker

During Ted's last year at Manchester College he explored organizations he could join as an alternative service worker. Bill Herod, a recruiter for Vietnam Christian Service visited Manchester College to talk about the organization's work in Vietnam. Ted was well aware of the ongoing destruction caused by the war so he had many questions regarding volunteer work in Vietnam. It was this organization that Ted decided to join after he would complete his upcoming graduate studies in social work. On June 12, 1967, he graduated from Manchester College with a BA degree in Sociology and Psychology.

A Message to the Home Church

The summer that Ted graduated from Manchester College he was asked to talk to his hometown church at the West Milton Church of the Brethren. On August 27, 1967 at 22 years of age he gave the following presentation.

For What It's Worth

There comes a time when a man needs to make his thoughts and ideas known, to express himself in all sincerity and honesty concerning the "important questions" of life. If there is to be meaning in life, I find there must be certain questions, certain beliefs, certain values and goals relentlessly pursued. At this maturing time in my life, I find there are certain thoughts and ideas which weigh rather heavily upon my mind. My views concerning the world, the church and Christian responsibility have been revamped and redefined since my participation in collegiate life activities during the past three years.

Just as our materialist world is constantly advancing and changing today, so have my personal beliefs and values changed and developed. Many forces have been at work during my numerous encounters at Manchester College. Students, friends, professors, ministers, books, term papers and hundreds of personal experiences have all had a significant part to play in making me the person I am today.

I am told that Socrates once said, "Knowledge is ignorance." I think it was only after I had spent some time at Manchester that I began to understand the meaning of this seemingly contradictory statement. For the more knowledge I gained, the more I began to realize how much I really didn't know; how small my insights really were; how lacking I was in true understanding. Knowledge is a joyous adventure, but it is also a terrible awakening, for me it means loss of innocence. For me, there is no substitute for the open-minded person searching for truth and a clearer understanding into all situations, one who is not afraid of an idea, one who is constantly searching for truth and a clearer understanding into all situations and one who is not afraid or ashamed to take a stand for what he believes and knows to be right.

While I have this opportunity I feel the need to voice some personal opinions, to take a stand, and to make known some guiding principles in my life which I feel should be given careful consideration by each of you. For I am firmly of the belief that he who takes a stand is occasionally and even often wrong, but he who never takes a stand is always wrong.

When I accepted the invitation to speak here this morning I had some mixed feelings. I deeply wanted to express myself to the congregation, but I also realized my inexperience for such a sacred task as mounting the pulpit. Just what do these familiar faces expect from a "young whippersnapper" fresh out of college? Do I really have anything meaningful and worthwhile to say to my hometown congregation at the West Milton Church of the Brethren? And even if I did express myself, would the congregation really understand what I and the other students are trying to say? Can anyone ever fully understand another person until he has gone through similar experiences himself? These are questions which ran through my mind as I anticipated this Sunday morning. But once I had really thought about it, I realized my responsibility not only to the church, but to myself as well, to witness this morning for whatever value it may have.

While developing this message, a humorous analogy crossed my mind. It was about an old chicken that stopped in the middle of the road—because she wanted to "lay it on the line." Although I don't feel I've stopped in the middle of the road, I do feel that I'm at a crucial point in my life. But I too would like to lay some of my concerns on the line for what they're worth.

Before some would jump to the conclusion that I may be unjustly negative and critical, let me be quick to justify myself. It is rather difficult to objectively evaluate the effects of the church or education, on a person's life. I think it is often easier to devaluate and criticize than to praise. John Baldwin, the famous black author, once said, "Because I have such a great love for this country, I feel the responsibility to be continuously critical of her." I think this idea pretty well sums up my feelings toward the church. I love the church for helping to shape me into the kind of person I want to be. I value highly my upbringing in the Church of the Brethren tradition, especially my acquired beliefs of our pacifistic stand.

I question some of the dogmatic practices associated with our church, but I also question some of the attitudes and motives of those who would be so quick to make radical changes. It concerns me that the teachings of the church often have not been put to use even within the church itself, let alone in the home, or out on the job. The old expression of the "Sunday Christian" is a rather trite and well-worn expression which I don't intend to belabor, but it does hold some truth. Why is the Church of the Brethren not increasing in numbers? Why don't our young people stay with the church when they mature?

It is my conviction that if the church is to remain a meaningful and worthwhile force in the world today, it needs to take a good, long, critical and constructive look at itself. We all realize the great speed with which our world is changing and advancing. Technology moves on; our hold of knowledge has doubled in the last ten years, and our fast moving society waits for no man to fritter away his time, but what about our religion? What about our church? Does it not also need to keep open to change, to new ideas, to meeting the concerns and needs of people here and now?

Last month I made an interesting little empirical study for a psychology course I had at the college. For this study I devised and administered an interview schedule with which I questioned thirty youth ages 16 and 17 on their religious needs and opinions. It proved to be a very interesting study. One of the questions I asked was: "If you could do anything to change the church today, what would you do?" One youth answered, "I would take it out of the church and put it out into the streets where the real work of the church needs to be done." When asked what she would do to change the church today, a very intelligent fourth-generation Brethren girl quickly answered, "I would destroy the church," a rather startling reply, to say the least. But she went on to say that the church keeps people in ignorance of life as it really is, it encourages a false piety and it makes them satisfied with a "nice feeling" inside they get from attending church, which often serves more as a social function rather than a spiritual function.

Perhaps these youth have something significant to say, for they too had a great love and appreciation for the church, but they also realized it was an institution that could do a much more effective job.

Having eyes, we often do not see the meaning of Christ's example; having ears we do not hear the cries of those who await an honest friend; having sound minds and healthy bodies, we do not put faith into action when the action gets a bit tough and when there seems to be no reward for acting like a Christian.

Perhaps this idea of Christian behavior is really not such an impossible task as it may sound. I'd like to relate a little incident which comes rather close to home. These men didn't give me permission to use their names, but I'll reckon with them later if they object. This little incident took place after a live wire Sunday school discussion, downstairs in one of the classes which I attended when I was home last December, I believe. The discussion was very good and several ideas were exchanged. I forget exactly what was being discussed but after the class was over, I overheard Max Loxley and Joe Gosnell continue to discuss a few matters. Then I heard these men say something I suppose I'll never forget. Max said, "Well, if I can't quite agree with you, Joe, I sure respect you for saying what you think." And replying, Joe said, "If I can't still love you as a person, if I can't accept and respect you as a Christian brother even in our little disagreements, I've missed the whole purpose of being here." Now this is just one slight, seemingly insignificant conversation, but this gets right at the heart of Christianity for me, the idea that people are able to open themselves up to new ideas, to discuss concerns honestly and openly, and come out loving each other all the more for it.

It concerns me today that we are more willing to give up a little money and material goods than we are to give of ourselves, of our time, of our whole self for advancing the life which Christ set before us. It's easier to drop an envelope in the offering plate, easier to give some of the clothes we don't need anyway to needy people, but what about giving ourselves? There is still no substitute for face to face relationships, when man meets man honestly and openly. The work of the church requires lots of time and effort from many people if it intends to really do business. Too many times I find myself answering the call like so many others in the church. "Don't bug me." Don't bother me, brother, I'm too busy. I don't have time. I don't have the ability. I'll give some money if that will help, but not myself." And I thought about this matter when I was debating about my responsibility to the church. Certainly there are lots of other things I could be doing; it's a long way home, but how in the world could I be concerned with others who don't give themselves and their time if I don't do it myself. And so I've gotten much personal enjoyment and some real meaningful experiences from organizing and delivering worship services through college deputation teams, teaching Sunday school classes, and offering myself and my thoughts concerning the important questions of life.

I've found that many college students do a great deal more thinking about religious questions than most people realize; especially on a campus like Manchester. Discussion about religion, theology and philosophy is not uncommon between students, professors and counselors, especially as it relates to world affairs and life here and now. I've spent many hours discussing with roommates such questions as our belief in God, the shortcomings and strong points of the church today, or perhaps we'll get a discussion going about war and peace, or about a magazine article or a book concerning morality.

Now that I think about it, I don't know whether I've gained more from hours of meaningful personal discussion with friends or from my actual course work at the college. One example comes to mind. Myself and a few roommates were discussing books of the Bible which we thought spoke to most of us. I was telling how I liked Job because I remember from my Old Testament class that it was one of the books that really held meaning for me. My roommate was telling how he liked James. This may sound a little unusual, but he brought in the "good book" and read the whole book of James to me which was not a very long story, and I liked it too because it talks about a faith based on action. From our little discussion grew some very meaningful experiences and I got so excited about that particular book that I once developed and delivered a sermon around the ideas I got from James.

I guess I've begun to understand what Dr. Reiman meant when he said, "If you don't get a jolt when you read the Bible, if it doesn't really shock you, then you're not reading it right. Having studied quite a bit of sociology and psychology, I'm concerned about the effect of the church on a person's overt behavior and on his attitudes. For if our Christian religion doesn't express itself in our actions, in our thoughts and in our everyday relationships, I think we've missed the whole purpose of it all.

Recently I spoke at a very unique worship service for campers held outside by the Tippecanoe River in Northwestern Indiana. After the service I was approached by a lady who seemed very interested in talking and pursuing more of my thoughts as we exchanged ideas. Then she put a question to me that really sort of caught me off guard. She asked me plainly and simply if I had "met Christ personally." Now how do you answer a question like that, because if I would have said yes, I might have been lying, and had I said no, well I probably would have wished I had said yes to confirm my religiosity? At any rate I answered her by offering this little story which I once heard Dr. T. Wayne Reiman tell. It seems there was a very staunch and strict Church of the Brethren gentleman from Pennsylvania named Mr. Blocker. Once upon a time brother Blocker was questioned about his religiosity. Now I personally think it is rather presumptuous for anyone to stand in judgment concerning another's beliefs, nevertheless, Mr. Blocker was approached and asked very straight forwardly: "Brother, are you saved?" And Brother Blocker looked at him and said, "Ask my wife; ask my neighbors; ask the fellow where I work; ask the grocer."

And so this was the little story I told that inquisitive lady with the idea in mind that our religion is exhibited in our behavior, in our actions, in our relationships with others. And this behavior is on display every time we come in contact with another human being, be it your husband, your daughter, another member of the church, a stranger, or whoever. When we can really live our religion, when we can honestly love our neighbor as ourselves, then I think things would really begin to pop—our reasons for being here would take on new purpose and meaning.

I'm concerned this morning that man is increasingly trying to play God. Man is making God into his own image instead of visa-versa. God is dead, say some of our most learned theologians, and the shocking thing about it is that in many ways they're right. God is dead today for a good many people. If God is honesty and sincerity, if God exists in right human relationships, if God really is love and concern for our fellowman, then these men are pecking at the truth. Pick up the newspaper and what can you find? Riots in American cities, war in Southeast Asia, crime and delinquency, broken homes and broken human relationships. God is increasingly being edged out of the world as Bonhoeffer put it. I think every Christian has to face the ultimate question sometime, just who or what is God, and what does it all mean to me. Believe me, this question hits many conscientious minded Christian college students pretty hard after a year or two at Manchester. But this is a real blessing I think that many young people are provided the opportunity to meet and grapple with new ideas, and to find out for themselves just which road they will take in life.

What is God like? Look at Christ. Look at all Christ stood for, his mission on earth, his teachings, his actions, and his example. This for me is what God must be like. As I view world happenings today, I'm concerned about man's inhumanity to man. I think man needs desperately to concern himself more with his fellowman in this advancing machine age. Schweitzer writes, "As soon as man begins to reflect upon himself and his relationships with others, he becomes aware that men as such are his equals and his neighbors. The ethics of reverence for life requires that all of us enhance life, not hinder life."

(Holding up a picture of a starving, homeless child, a victim of the war) The newspaper article read: "Hunting was good today in the Mekong Delta region. U.S. Marines bagged 45 of the enemy, wounded scores, and completely wiped out one small village."

Hunting was good today! Just like the sportsman who comes back from a day of rabbit and pheasant hunting. He reaches into his hunting coat and pulls out the game he's bagged for the day! So many rabbits, so many pheasants and he lays them out for all to see. Only this time it's human lives that are bagged. The dehumanizing process of war concerns me deeply. What can I do about man's inhumanity to man?

We live in a society that spends more money for liquor, cigarettes and drugs than it does on education, a society that can spend billions for war preparation and yet calls itself a peace-loving nation. We live in a world that knows more about war than it does about peace; more about killing than it does about living. And it concerns me today that some people, important people in high offices and positions are so mistaken about how to live with their fellow man; sincerely mistaken.

Perhaps what I've said this morning is just old stuff. So what about it? What do I prescribe? I think the answer lies within each individual. I have a great respect and faith in the ability of each individual to face these important questions and concerns of life and to seek out meaningful answers. As Victor Frankl puts it, "Life ultimately means taking the responsibility to find the right answers to its problems, and to fulfill the tasks which it constantly sets before each individual."

And these words from the Prophet Micah speak to me just now, "For he has showed you, O man, what is right, and what does the Lord require of you, but to do justice, to love kindness and to walk humbly with your God." The apostle Paul told us, "When I was a child, I spoke and thought and reasoned as a child does. But when I became a man, my thoughts grew far beyond those of my childhood, and now I have put away the childish things."

So this is the way I feel this morning; these are my thoughts and my concerns for what they're worth. Good people of the West Milton Church of the Brethren, my home church, "Here I stand, God helping me, I can do no other."

Ted asked his audience to consider their own beliefs on issues of man's inhumanity to man and to ponder ways they can become personally accountable beyond passive acceptance of injustice. He posed the scenario, "When we can really live our religion, when we can honestly love our neighbor as ourselves, things will begin to pop." Going directly to some solutions to these challenging areas, he posed the question, "What is God like? Look at Christ. Look at all Christ stood for, his mission on earth, his teachings, his actions and his examples. This for me is what God must be like." Whether his listeners agreed or not, the implications of his presentation left the listeners with no other response than to at least consider the depth of his thoughts and the realities of his message.

It is noteworthy that years after Ted gave this presentation; portions of it continue to be referenced on various occasions by writers and other voices. They have described the issues that Ted addressed as timely and relevant throughout the passing years. They have also noted Ted's articulation clarity as well as his understanding of the power of God. This is a reality that he pointed to several times as he addressed the church.

Having grown up in the Church of the Brethren, Ted was aware of his Church's position on peace and the work to promote peace and justice as presented in the following timeline of the church's significant landmarks toward peace.

Date	Church of the Brethren Peace Timeline
1778	Christopher Sauer II was the owner of a religious German printing business. He settled in Pennsylvania, printed pacifist materials and spread the message of nonviolent peace. His property was confiscated and sold at public auction because he was a pacifist.
1864	John Kline (1797-1864) was a Church of the Brethren minister who traveled by horseback to preach the gospel in several states in the east and Midwest. During the Civil War he traveled in areas loyal to both the Union and Confederate sides. He refused to participate in military service. He spoke and wrote about his nonviolent beliefs in letters, publications and in the pulpit. In 1862 he was put in jail for two weeks for his conscientious objection to military service. In 1864 while traveling home from church annual conference, John was killed by Confederate soldiers. In his diary he stated that he would die rather than to disobey God by taking up arms.
1911	A peace committee was established at annual conference.
1918	Annual conference in Goshen, Indiana passes a statement against military service. It was later withdrawn due to government pressure.
1939	Heifers for Relief Committee considers ways to implement the vision of Dan West to address the world's hunger problem.
1939	Brethren Service Committee established to: • bring assistance and rehabilitation to the people affected by war • direct conscientious objectors to perform civilian service • manage volunteers in service projects throughout the world • supply food and humanitarian aid
1940	Conscientious objectors for the first time are accepted by the government and are exempted from military service.

Date	Church of the Brethren Peace Timeline
1941	Church of the Brethren joins the Federal Council of Churches (later known as the World Council of Churches) for the purpose of feeding, clothing, providing medical aid, and care for the aging and shelter for the homeless.
1941	The Brethren Service Commission was established. As a result of this organization Brethren Disaster Services were developed to provide physical and material assistance as needed after disasters.
1942	Heifer Project, founded by Dan West, becomes an official program of the Brethren Service Committee. Instead of providing a container of milk to a family in need of food, a cow is given to the family. Recipients promise to donate the first female calf to another family to meet their hunger needs. The program quickly grew and broadened its scope. By 1944 the name was changed to Heifer International. A large variety of animals were added as well as sustainable agriculture strategies and training. By the mid-1970s it was necessary for Heifer International to have several farms for their animals including a 1,200 acre ranch in Arkansas. Besides addressing global hunger, this organization provides people with dignity, training and an opportunity to "pass on the gift of life."
1944	Brethren Service Commission obtains the property of the Blue Ridge College at New Windsor, Maryland. From this location, world service projects are established: • A conference center • Headquarters for processing clothing for shipment to people in need • Headquarters for SERRV International, an organization with the purpose of eradicating poverty by supporting artisans and farmers worldwide by purchasing and marketing their products • On Earth Peace Assembly. A staff of volunteers who help groups of people grow in peace by providing skills, support and spiritual foundations for overcoming violence with the power of love.
1948	Brethren Volunteer Service was created to train people before sending them out to serve human needs and the cause of peace through various life sustaining projects around the world. Volunteers work in such areas as agriculture, construction, health, teaching, economic development and child care. BVS also trains volunteers for church leadership and personal growth experiences.
1952	The Brethren, Mennonite and Quaker Churches lobby for the Selective Service Act. It provides for the deferment of conscientious objectors through a program of alternative service.
1953	International Voluntary Service is founded by Mennonite, Brethren and Quaker Churches. They provide NGO volunteer service to third world countries including Laos, Vietnam and Cambodia. This organization dissolved in 2002.

Date	Church of the Brethren Peace Timeline
1957	The Church of the Brethren presents their position on war: "We believe that good citizenship extends beyond our own national boundaries and will therefore serve to remove the occasions for war. Convinced that good citizens in a good society must work out a better way than war to resolve international conflict, we have in recent years undertaken a diligent search for practical and effective means to that end."
1971	Ted Studebaker is killed by forces opposing the American military on April 26, 1971 while serving as a conscientious objector in Vietnam through Vietnam Christian Service.
1979	Brethren Disaster Ministries focuses on rebuilding homes, caring for children, and providing international relief by engaging volunteers, supporters and partners to serve communities recovering from disaster.

It was Ted's vision to eventually become a social worker. Accordingly he considered graduate schools to earn a master of social work degree which he would need for an eventual vocation in social work. In September of 1967 Ted traveled to Florida where he was accepted into the Florida State University School of Social Welfare. He had applied for and was awarded a grant from the state of Alabama Department of Mental Health for living and tuition expenses throughout his graduate studies program. The contract stated that Ted shall work one month for the Alabama Department of Mental Health for each month he receives financial assistance. The grant provided Ted with the finances he would need to reach another milestone, that of becoming a social worker. Once again, his steps to achieve these goals showed thoughtful financial planning.

One of Ted's Practicum experiences at Florida State University was working with patients at a mental health clinic. This experience gave him a grasp of some of the challenges faced by administering to the needs of mentally ill patients. He expressed his desire to work in this area.

While pursuing his studies Ted made friends with several of his peers who were in the social work program. They had worked as a group on some of the assignments. They became further acquainted through social gatherings. Occasionally some of the men in the group played touch football together on Saturdays which was a welcome break from their rigorous assignments. On some occasions Ted and his friends met socially where Ted entertained them with guitar music. On March 21, 1969, Ted graduated from Florida State University with a Master of Social Work degree.

Joel Freedman, one of Ted's friends in the social work program (MSW) at Florida State University had the following reflections about Ted.

> I believe Ted's spirituality remains alive and relevant in my own life. I believe it was more than coincidental that on a day in 1981 that I took action to stop a harmful addiction. That day was also the 10th anniversary of Ted's death. It helps to feel connected to others, living or deceased, who have traveled similar paths. I can still sense Ted reminding me not to give up on causes I believe in. To this day I regard Ted as one of my guarding angels.
>
> At a time when our country seems to have become a battleground between human spirituality and the forces of indifference and non-caring, I often think about my friend Ted Studebaker and everything he stood for.
>
> At school (Florida State University) we all knew Ted for his warm smile and easy going manner. He liked to sing and play the guitar. It was an amazing and humbling experience to begin to realize that the social concerns which Ted had tried to spark with just what little he could do in an isolated spot, instead of being suddenly cut off, were somehow spreading and growing. His ideals reflect the finest qualities of human spirituality. Such qualities must not be lost in today's difficult times.
>
> Joel

Another of Ted's friends at Florida State University was Lou Pagliuca. He and Ted were in the same social work study group for a period of time. Lou made these observations about his relationship with Ted.

> My memories of Ted are quite clear. He was a quiet and reserved man, but not without opinions and a philosophy of life. He, as was everyone else, devoted to the welfare of his fellowman and he was quite caring about people. Clearly my New York accent was dramatically different than his Midwest enunciation, but I initially thought he was from the south. He spoke softly, slowly and with reserve. He chose his words deliberately to keep from imposing his views and values on others and being offensive. He never did offend anyone and I found his outlook and opinions refreshing.
>
> He always maintained a smile and was respectful of those around him no matter the vast differences among all of us. Without question he was an intelligent and kind man. I got to know even more about Ted when our group would gather on weekends near the football stadium to play touch football. It was here that I found Ted to be an exceptional athlete and more aggressive than

his otherwise genteel manner would have suggested. He could run, was strong and an overall very good athlete who enjoyed the physicality of sports. Although Ted was not a physically imposing and large man, he played with great strength and endurance. Never did he try to hurt anyone.

I remember vividly the time we were playing and I attempted to run through a fellow student who stood 6' 4" tall and weighed at least 325 pounds (a foolish thing to try at my 5' 9" and 130 pound frame). When I finally regained consciousness after about 5 minutes, there was Ted the first to inquire if I was okay.

These weekend warrior sports outings were a vital complement to our studies about human nature. I got to know him as much from these times as from the classroom and came to see him as a well-rounded individual.

Whenever classmates got together for other social gatherings, Ted would bring his guitar and entertain us by singing popular songs of the era, as well as songs he had written. This was a side of Ted we came to know and enjoy. His songs were of peace, justice and hope as he addressed the chaos of the world. Without a doubt, Ted was a multi-talented man who had deep convictions about the world we live in. He was opposed to war and man's cruelty to man and I was not surprised when I learned that he went to Vietnam with a church group to fight a different kind of battle.

After graduation and for the next 22 years, I was a Clinical Social Work Officer in the United States Air Force, working primarily in mental health clinics in the United States and two foreign countries. I too chose to address human suffering by helping military members and their families who were struggling with the various effects of military life including war. I did not keep in touch with Ted after graduation from Florida State as all of us went our separate ways to "do the world good."

Needless to say, I was shocked when I heard the news of Ted's passing in Vietnam. How could this man of peace be taken by the very thing he strongly opposed? Through the many years that have passed I have never forgotten Ted Studebaker, the things he strongly believed in and the kind and gentle man he was. If you were to ask any of our classmates, every one of them would remember Ted Studebaker in the same light I am sharing.

Lou

Chapter 4

Volunteer Service

"I don't want to be remembered as the girl who was shot. I want to be remembered as the girl who stood up."

—MALALA YOUSAFZAI

WITHIN DAYS AFTER GRADUATING from Florida State University, Ted went to New Windsor, Maryland (April 7, 1969) where he began training through Brethren Volunteer Service (BVS). He was a member of the 83rd BVS unit with 26 volunteers in his training unit. The training provided sessions to equip the volunteers with skills they would need for their upcoming volunteer service assignments. Training was provided through discussion groups, guest speakers, and by providing leadership responsibilities at a local church. The New Windsor location was also a worldwide processing center for clothing donations. One of the responsibilities of the BVS unit was the work of processing clothing for distribution to those in need throughout the world.

Ted's BVS experiences also included the following activities:

- Group interaction sessions called "See Groups:" These sharing sessions provided the members with an opportunity to develop skills in listening, expressing themselves and contributing to the group discussion process. The exchange in these sessions can become intense with personal accountability exposed as participants express their feelings and find ways to problem solve and build rapport. Ted described these experiences as "insightful."

- Ministry participation: Ted took an interest in teaming with his peers to plan and carry out a Sunday worship service at a local church where he and Don Snyder, the BVS director, spoke to the congregation. Don spoke on the topic of service and Ted's presentation dealt with peacemaking.

- Guitar music: On several occasions Ted provided guitar music and singing for chapel services and during leisure time in the evenings.

- Sports and recreation: In the early morning Ted and his friends took time to work out through physical activities of cross country and a variety of recreational activities.

- Speakers: Guest speakers sparked Ted's interest. They included Clarence Jordan a farmer and New Testament Greek scholar who was instrumental in founding Habitat for Humanity. He also authored the Cotton Patch translation of the New Testament. Other speakers who interested Ted were Tom Martin from the Resister's Movement. Tom engaged the group in a discussion on peace through nonviolence.

- A day at the Bruderhoff: This is a Christian community movement inspired by the example of the first church in Jerusalem as described in the New Testament. Bruderhoff communities relinquish self-interest for the sake of the common good. They seek to promote nonviolence, faithfulness and compassion for the poor.

As Ted was nearing the end of his BVS training, he received a letter with his official acceptance into Vietnam Christian Service. He followed up by making a phone call to the VNCS organization to make further preparation to leave for Vietnam. He anticipated his new assignment and responsibilities with enthusiasm. His diary entry stated, "Oh how soon can I go. I find myself losing touch here, maybe on purpose." He said his final goodbyes to his BVS friends on May 4th, 1969. "It was a great BVS encounter," he stated, "sad to leave but happy to move on." His volunteer service pay of $30.00 per month may have seemed small, but Ted like many other volunteers viewed this service as a welcome and essential part of life. Assisting people in need in under developed countries was a calling that needed to be fulfilled.

Vietnam Christian Service

His departure for Vietnam began on May 7th 1969. He flew from New York City to Chicago where he met with Church of the Brethren officials in the Elgin, Illinois offices. He received their words of support and called his parents for a last goodbye. His flight to Saigon took him by way of Chicago, Anchorage, Tokyo and Hong Kong.

Ted in Elgin, IL before departing for Vietnam

When he arrived in Hong Kong on May 10, 1969, his luggage was missing. It was in Hong Kong that Ted observed the differences between extreme wealth and poverty. He commented on the vast array of merchandise for sale in the shops. "So much to buy, but I can do without it. Who needs a camera, tape recorder, radio or any such gadget? Why should I have such luxuries if those I'll work with, don't. I'll practice moderation. Here I eat while children starve. Soon I will give instead of just getting."

Chapter 5

Saigon

"The path to true non-violence requires much more courage than violence."
—MAHATMA GANDHI

Ted's journal entries

May 12, 1969

Washed my clothes before boarding a flight bound for Saigon. I was met at the Saigon airport by Bob Miller, the director of VNCS. Luggage is still missing. Visited Vietnam Orphanage. Heat and traffic at Saigon Airport are unforgettable. A real hell hole, but I grit my teeth, for I know I can do the job. Got acquainted with the VNCS office and staff in Saigon.

May 13, 1969

Still no luggage. Tired from the heat and mental strain of the cultural shock so I slept well. A million books are no substitute for the real encounter in Saigon. Filled out bunches of forms, read lots of materials. Getting oriented with Church World Service (CWS) people in Saigon. VNCS people begin to seem a little more human. I'm coming around too. Starting to listen to language tapes.

May 14, 1969

Still no luggage. Listening to language tapes again. This is going to be tough but I can do the job. Crowded housing in Saigon but the people seem amazingly humble and elastic.

May 15, 1969

Still no luggage. I'm coming around, starting to recover from the cultural shock. Met Pakdy (also known as Lee Ven Pak), a cute Chinese girl. She and I started language training together.

May 16, 1969

Still no luggage. Went to airport to explain the luggage problem. Volleyball, swimming, socialized with VNCSers, played guitar and we sang. Language training in the morning. Surprisingly excellent health, slept well. Getting to know other VNCSers.

May 17, 1969

Language training in the morning. Visited more of Saigon with VNCSers.

May 18, 1969

Went to Catholic Church in Downtown Saigon. Very flat ritualistic service. Language study.

May 19, 1969

Reviewing language, vowels, consonant sounds and tones.

Got my luggage today (9 days later). Air Vietnam found it in To-kyo. Playing guitar, felt good. I need to buckle down and study more and most important, be humble always, Micah 6:8. Mr. Cook reviewed VNCS goals and philosophy with us.

May 21, 1969

The military has corrupted everything here in Vietnam. I feel very lucky, very undeserving of the luxury of VNCS training, hous-ing, food, etc. Here I eat while some children starve. Soon I will give instead of just getting. Language study is going well. I went through lesson in one day instead of one week. I really have fun with the Vietnam teachers. Playing guitar and singing with VNC-Sers. Great time. Read letter from Miss Dickey (his hometown first grade teacher). Got driver's license. The qualities of humility and humor are great assets. I enjoy the Vietnamese people very much. Played volleyball in the PM.

On the first day of language training in Saigon, Ted met Pakdy a Chinese classmate who had come from Hong Kong to serve in Vietnam through Asian Christian Service. As they became acquainted and practiced language together, Ted was attracted to her and they soon developed a friendship.

In less than one month after arriving in Saigon, Ted obtained his license for operating a motorbike. He was pleased to be navigating with the VNCS Lambretta Motorbike on the busy streets of Saigon. One day he asked Pakdy if she would like to take a ride with him to see the scenes in Saigon. This became a routine each day after language class. The spacious Saigon Zoo was one of the several places they visited. Pakdy said she was happy that Ted took notice of her as they continued their growing relationship.

For one of their language classes the students went with their teacher to a restaurant to practice their Vietnamese where they ordered pho, a Vietnamese noodle soup consisting of broth, linguine-shaped rice noodles, a few herbs, and meat. Ted also sharpened his Vietnamese speaking skills by practicing with the children who lived near the VNCS house. One day when he visited them they were using their sling shot with amazing accuracy which was intriguing to Ted. "One kid shot a sparrow out of a tree 60 feet away with a sling shot. Wow, I never saw anything like it. He acted as if it was nothing. I admire his modesty."

Realizing how critical language acquisition was to making friends and implementing agriculture projects, Ted was highly motivated to learn to speak Vietnamese. He carried a pocket-size notebook with him to write words and their pronunciation which he frequently practiced with the local people.

At the end of the eight-week language training class, Ted was assigned to work in agriculture projects in Di Linh in the Central Highlands of Vietnam. Pakdy was assigned child care responsibilities with refugees in Tuy Hoa, a coastal town 200 miles northeast of Di Linh. Travel time between these two towns was 7 ½ hours by bus. The separation brought tears of sadness to Pakdy, but Ted assured her that he would write to her so they kept in touch by mail. Pakdy also sent Ted some sweaters that she had knitted and some flower drawings she had made. During their two year assignments at these locations Pakdy used her holidays to visit Ted on several occasions. Ted and Pakdy also visited when they attended VNCS meetings in Saigon. When they occasionally saw one another, they continued their conversation and learned more about each other's beliefs and interests.

Prior to doing volunteer work for Asian Christian service, Pakdy was a secretary for an American missionary in Hong Kong for about two years. She also had experience working in a library in Hong Kong for about two years. These experiences were helpful to her when she began work for Asian Christian Service where she was offered an opportunity to do child-care work with refugee children. She also had the thought that she might be able to meet a nice American in Vietnam and get married.

Chapter 6

Di Linh

"The most important assistance we offer is accompaniment. If people in dire circumstances know we are walking with them, they may gain some sense of security—maybe this is passing the peace."

—JERRY AAKER

PHYLLIS CRIBBY DESCRIBED HER nursing work in the Di Linh area, the environment, the culture and traditions of the Montagnards at the time she and Ted were VNCS colleagues in Di Linh:

> The early morning view from our house in Di Linh looks very peaceful as do many spots in this beautiful country. These hills are the territory of the Montagnards, a tribal people whose ancestors are believed to have originated in the upper Mekong Valleys of China. They migrated here many centuries ago. But now there are other occupants in these mountains. Just to one side of this scene, an ARVN battalion is camped and somewhere out there are Viet Cong guerrillas. The Montagnards are caught in the middle, between the ARVN and the Viet Cong, between animism and Christianity, between illiteracy and education. There is a younger generation who are seeking to depart from traditional farming to the world of science and technology.
>
> I am working in a health care clinic program in Montagnard villages. Although the Vietnamese government has a public health department, its work in these villages is mainly concerned with immunizations and control of epidemics. There is no government mobile clinic program. Each village has one or more resident

village health workers who have received six weeks training and are supposed to have a stock of basic medicines and supplies for dressings. When patients require increased care in the hospital they are trained to refer such cases. However, there are many problems that make such medical care problematic. Hospitals are often far away and transportation is difficult. Some people have bicycles and motor bikes but no four wheeled vehicles and buses are constantly overcrowded. Due to tribal beliefs about sickness and death the people rarely seek hospital treatment on their own.

During the time I have been in Di Linh, there has been no doctor in the hospital here. However, a Vietnamese doctor has been assigned to the hospital this month. Medicines in the villages are usually incomplete or non-existent. The clinic buildings are often damaged by the war or the weather and the workers are sometimes unavailable. Consequently, there are many neglected or unmet health needs in the villages. Our program seeks to help meet these needs and promote utilization of these government facilities when possible.

Most Montagnard health workers are men. K'Chuong is a Montagnard male nurse who has had one year of training in Ban Me Thuout. K'Lai prepares patients' record cards and writes their histories and symptoms. Co Son, a Vietnamese social worker does follow-up home visits. K'Chuong and I examine patients, give out medications and provide dressings. We try to take all serious cases to a hospital but often the people will refuse to go especially when they think they are dying. It is very important to them that they die in their home. Plague, malaria and tuberculosis are high incident medical conditions here. Intestinal parasites, skin infection and fungi are constant problems also. We also see victims of unexploded ammunition.

All aspects of tribal life are governed by customs and are dominated by religion. Ritualistic traditions are passed from generation to generation. There are special rules for building houses, preparing food, cultivating and planting the fields. Those who deviate from tradition are subject to great disapproval. The village chief is chosen for his knowledge of tribal tradition, not for physical strength or wealth. A vast pantheon of spirits are involved in the animalistic beliefs. Successful interaction with these spirits is accomplished through appropriate rituals, ceremonies, taboos, interdictions and sacrifices. Sacrifices are offered for births, death, illness, special occasions and for violation of taboos. The buffalo is considered the prime sacrificial animal. Pigs, goats and chickens are used for secondary sacrifices. Animals are raised chiefly for sacrifices. Although buffalo are used for cultivation of wet lands in the valleys neither buffalo or goats are milked. However, the meat of a sacrificial animal is eaten and since sacrifices are frequently made (if animals are available); there is no protein deficiency in this area.

Evil spirits are believed to cause illness. If the family can afford it, a sorcerer or sorceress is called to determine the proper spirit to be invoked and the sacrifices necessary to restore health. The drastic upheavals in living patterns necessitated by the war has caused some loosening of tribal practices.

There are eighteen main tribal divisions in Vietnam and many sub-tribes. The Koho is one of the largest groups. The distinct groups among the Koho have such closely related dialects that communication among them is possible. Through their travels, some have also acquired an understanding of the languages of neighboring tribes and some have also learned to speak Vietnamese through trade and other contacts. The Koho dialects consist mostly of short monosyllabic words and the vocabulary is limited.

There is no indigenous Koho written language, but American missionaries have developed one and lesson books have been prepared for teaching Koho literacy which is still low. There is a strong oral tradition of sharing proverbs, riddles and legends. Humorous stories are transmitted in rhythmic, poetic form.

Most of the Koho society is matrilineal. The extended family and the village are the two most important social units. Families live in nuclear units. Large families are wanted and the women often bear twelve or more children, however infant mortality is high. Female children are preferred but there is no great emphasis on this. Orphans are usually cared for by the mother's family although sometimes neighbors adopt them and care for them like their own children.

Education is not compulsory in Vietnam but there are government schools. Secondary and higher has the requirement of passing graduated tests which are all in Vietnamese. Therefore, Montagnards who want to complete their education must first learn a second language. For two years VNCS has operated a school in a Montagnard section of Di Linh to teach the children to read and write their own language (Koho) and to introduce them to Vietnamese so they can go to elementary school.

It is quite a joyful experience for me to visit the school. I try to go several times a month to check on health problems, provide first aid and give health lessons. The children are bright and eager to learn.

Phyllis Cribby
February 1971

When Ted arrived in Di Linh he spent one week being oriented by Gayle Preheim, the person whom he would be replacing. Gayle took Ted to the various agriculture projects in Di Linh and the surrounding towns. Ted asked many questions regarding the feasibility of making progress with the agriculture projects, the war, the people, their acceptance of VNCS workers, etc.

Gayle Preheim

In the short time that Ted and I were together in Di Linh, I sensed, though only understood later, that there was something special about him. I remember him asking me one day how I decided what kind of projects and programing I had decided to do. I was the unit leader, so I was the obvious person to ask. I remember being surprised by his question. I didn't have an answer for him. He did not press me, just planted the seed; although, I am sure he was thinking about concepts such as assessment, cultural implications, partnering, community, etc. Later, I got it. I got lots of stuff after I left Vietnam.

Green off the farm with only a bachelor's degree and away from home, I was very geared into producing bigger and better. I was into program development, the more the better. Looking at my journal, by the time Ted arrived, I wasn't even taking time to be reflective-only two journal entries between May and August my last summer. I felt like I had a tiger by the tail. Sadly, the very time I would have benefited the most from taking time to be with the people, to be contemplative about what I had and was experiencing, was lost by western bigger-is-better mentality. Only in the years following as I took time to look back and reflect did I realize that our Vietnamese and Montagnard friends did not talk about the programming of those who had preceded us. They spoke of the persons, of who they were and what they stood for, of their personalities, of their friendship. I think Ted knew that when he came. His professional training aside, what Ted brought was that intangible sense of self who understood and related at a much deeper level than most of the rest of us ever could.

During the time I got to know Ted, I saw him connect with the local people in an extraordinary way. His openness and warmth radiated in his personality. I saw people drawn to him, as weren't we all. Cultural barriers dropped as Ted moved in his environment. In fact, because I saw that Ted would have tremendous influence in his community during his time there, I initially wondered when I received word that he had been killed, whether his presence and work with the Montagnards became a threat to the Vietnamese government to the point where they might have orchestrated his assassination to make it look like a VC murder. I could not conceive of anyone wanting to take the life of this gentle, loving person. I do hope that what really happened was more along the lines of what you and we heard when we were in Di Linh-that Ted lost his life through a series of tragic circumstances that unfolded the way they did for reasons that are hard to understand.

Gayle Preheim
May 28, 2012

Ted deeply appreciated Gayle's humility and friendship and was reluctant to see Gayle leave at the end of one week when his two year period of service had come to an end. In his journal Ted described his work as a catalyst. He understood he was not in Vietnam to do their work for them, therefore he knew he needed to be enterprising at finding what he could do and how he could best provide assistance with self-help projects.

Having just completed eight weeks of Vietnamese language training, it was time to begin learning the Koho language. Realizing how critical language acquisition is to making friends and receiving acceptance, Ted was highly motivated to speak Koho so he diligently spent time practicing the language. His Koho co-workers, K'Krah and K'Lai had experience as VNCS agriculture workers. It was these two men with whom Ted would coordinate for the agriculture projects. These were the men who assisted Ted in learning to speak the Koho language. Ted savored some of the peculiar phrases and on one occasion when writing home he shared a few translations. One of his choice phrases was the Koho greeting, Niam-Sa. "It literally means how is your body?"

K'Lai, Ted and K'Krah

As his schedule permitted, Ted attended the Tin Lanh Church, a Christian church in Di Linh where he participated in the church services conducted in the Koho language. This also gave him an opportunity to further grasp the Koho language. When he was in Saigon for meetings or training, he attended the International Protestant Church when his schedule permitted.

When Ted first arrived in Di Linh he shared the VNCS house with three other volunteers. They were: Jeanie Gutshall, a VNCS nurse, Daisy Benares, a rice expert working for International Voluntary Service and Terry Bonnet, the VNCS team leader.

About one year later (June 23, 1970), Phyllis Cribby arrived in Di Linh to replace Jeanie Gutshall, the VNCS nurse whose tour of service was ending. Daisy and Phyllis shared the same room in the VNCS house. Phyllis and Ted developed a trusting friendship. Their rapport was one of mutual respect and they enjoyed the camaraderie of discussing their respective assignments in the highlands. Phyllis provided health care services in Di Linh and several surrounding villages. She worked with health care aids and interpreters as she held clinics. She also kept individual health records, administered medications and presented lessons to the Koho people on various health issues. When necessary, Phyllis transported patients to the hospital.

Front: Ted with Pudden, the dog. Back: Phyllis Cribby and Terry Bonnet

The Koho are a maternal society and the children carry the family name of the mother. It is the tradition for the Koho girl to choose her husband. After marriage, the husband remains in his wife's village. All other issues are decided by the males of the village. A village leader or chief is elected to make decisions about their community and governmental affairs.

The main source of income among most of the Koho is derived from farming. Rice is their main crop but they also grow vegetables and fruit. Income from farming is meager and very few farmers have mechanized equipment. Accordingly, some of the Koho are among the poorest of the minority groups in the Central Highlands. To supplement their earnings, some of those with artistic skills engage in arts and crafts and have found ways to sell their products.

Many of the Koho and other hill tribe groups in the Central Highlands have been Christianized by missionaries in the early 1900s. Although the children are learning the Vietnamese language in school, the indigenous language is still spoken in most homes. Past forms of the Koho tradition are disappearing such as the original style of clothing, animist beliefs and ritual practices.

Ted was pleased that VNCS provided several agriculture training sessions in both crop and animal production. At one of the trainings held in the Saigon area he visited a poultry and swine farm. At another training he learned about planting, plowing and harvesting rice. One of his training sessions was held in Dalat on the subject of vegetable gardening from Taiwanese agriculture experts.

Ted in a rice test plot

Agriculture Projects

Ted continued the agriculture projects that Gayle had begun and he developed other projects as time, training and supplies became available. His agriculture work was in Di Linh as well as some of the nearby villages within a 6 mile radius. He described many disruptions and failures when implementing the agriculture projects. "Everything seems unstable, unpredictable and unworkable here in beautiful Vietnam. The rice test plots grew poorly compared to the local varieties. We had little or no results with the seeds we gave to the farmers, so I gave them to the Vietnamese gardeners in the valley below the VNCS house. I hope to learn a lot from these experts." On one occasion water buffalo got loose and damaged some of Ted's rice plots. On another day a mortar exploded in the rice plots and destroyed a portion of the crop. One night a mortar landed on Ted's sorghum plots and destroyed a portion of that crop. However, Ted commented, "The progress, no matter how small, seems to outweigh the negative experiences." Eventually he provided the following demonstration projects and services:

Chickens

Ted obtained baby chicks and found the safest place to protect them from the weather and keep them warm was in a discarded bathtub. At maturity the 12 chickens did well by averaging 8 or 9 eggs per day all together.

Ted caring for the baby chicks

Bees

"I purchased two hives of honey bees and bee keeping equipment. The bees did well for the first few months. Then one hive ate all their honey and left their hive. Some may have joined the remaining hive that is thriving."

Crops

Ted established experiment plots of rice, behind the VNCS house where he also had demonstration plots of beans, tomatoes and sorghum.

Hydraulic Ram

The hydraulic ram (hydram) was a project that Gayle Preheim had started. Ted wrote, "We have two hydram projects going, one in So Nam Village and we are planning for one in the Kaming Village. It will pump 4000 gallons of water per day. This calls for building a dam to hold back water in order to have a sufficient water fall to drive the pump. We just finished a big water storage tank for our hydram." This was an ongoing project that Ted intended to complete as time allowed. Gayle Preheim shared with Ted about his experience with the hydraulic ram:

> The hydraulic (hydram) pump was one of my projects which became known in VNCS circles as the "VNCS Edsel", after that famed Ford motor product that failed miserably. In fact, later when I was in graduate school, I used this example of how not to do community development. It all started with a memo from VNCS headquarters in Saigon that Oxfam, the well-known and well-healed, British philanthropic organization wanted to donate hydram pumps to VNCS. I was familiar with these pumps having seen one in operation at the source of an artisan well near my childhood farm home in SD. I remembered seeing a spring on a hillside near a Montagnard village. It was the perfect location for this pump. Additionally, the people of the village walked down into a valley where there was a well for their drinking water, to wash their clothes, etc. Because this pump uses the force of gravity as energy to lift water from a lower location to a higher location, we would be able to bring water directly into the village saving them all that work of going down to the creek to get water. In the summer of '69, about the time Ted arrived in Di Linh, this project was about to begin. All the supplies had been ordered

and delivered. We had one meeting with the village chief basically telling him what we planned to do and asking for some villagers to help carry supplies, build the water holding dam and the brick water tank up in the village, etc. It was a huge undertaking.

Finally, the project was done. Everything worked beautifully. We had a grand opening with the appropriate dignitaries, etc. Only, the people never used it. They continued walking past the water tank up in the village while on their way down into the valley below to get water, wash clothes-and socialize! The well, as I understood later, was the community gathering place, the nerve center of the village. That could not be moved. Obviously, we had not done the necessary assessment beforehand. I have thought often about that hydram pump perhaps still sitting on its concrete slab on that hillside rusting away. I learned the VC had autographed the pump. I'm sure they probably also had a good laugh at the Americans who bring their ethnocentrism to other countries.

Farm Machinery Training

Ted brought in a rice tiller and a rice huller with the help of his co-workers. With both of these farm implements the Koho farmers were able to spend less time tilling the fields and hulling the rice. Ted worked with K'Krah to train the local farmers on how to use and maintain this equipment.

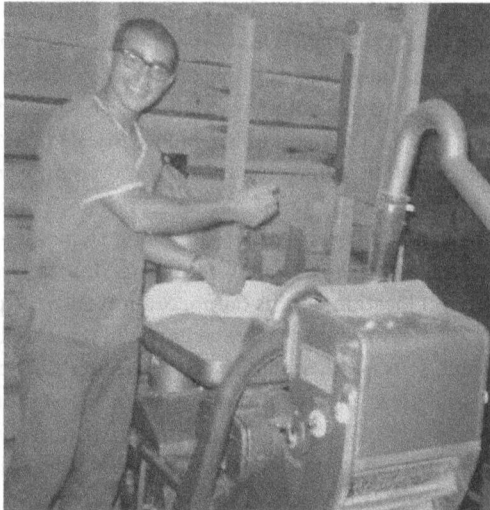

The new rice huller

Fish

A fish pond was started in the village of Gia Lanh but Ted described an unexpected problem. "We started a fish pond but all the fish died that we put in the pond." It was believed to have been contaminated soil, another disappointment. To assess their accountability and progress in the various projects, Ted wrote a monthly report and an evaluation of his projects and sent the reports to the VNCS office in Saigon. His assessments were comprehensive and they included suggestions for improvement to assist future volunteers.

Agriculture supplies

Since the farmers did not have transportation to get the supplies they needed, Ted bought fertilizer, fencing and other agriculture supplies that the farmers needed and sold them to the farmers at cost.

Failures

All of Ted's projects involved problem solving and intuitive resourcefulness to make equipment repairs, coordinate with his co-workers and communicate with the farmers. However, not all of the projects were free of difficulties. Jeanie noted that there were many frustrating experiences for Ted. When the people of Ka Ning found out that VNCS did not have enough tillers for them, they became angry and demanding. It happened again with the rice huller. The people seemed to expect and insist that all their rice be hulled first. Jeanie explained that many of Ted's projects raised the same questions—what programs work and how can they best be implemented? One time the honey combs were stolen from the hives. Vegetables planted in the garden were often stolen by ARVN soldiers and others. Other problems included machinery breakdowns, theft of agriculture items and difficulties getting the ram to work. Ted even experienced criticism from his own agriculture co-workers. These were problems he shared with Jeanie and confided in her as a colleague and VNCS co-worker.

During an interview, Howard Royer asked Ted to describe the major obstacles to his agriculture work: "Simply the war including the destruction, the death and the intrusion into the lives of everyone. The military has corrupted everything here in Vietnam." Ted described how fortunate some people are compared to others.

As distressful as some of these failures were, it was a strong desire for him to persist as best he could in an attempt to find solutions. His letters and diary notes give us a picture of the self-discipline he applied during these difficult times. His comments included the following:

- "Remember the good Lord rewards only effort not success."
- "I need to be more tolerant and accepting."
- "Careful, I'm down on too much too soon."
- "Think I ought to be a little more humble. I ain't thought of that too much lately."
- "I could have been more humble today. Lord maybe I need a kick in the pants."
- "I must apply self-discipline."

During the uplifting and encouraging times, when achievements were realized, a familiar journal entry would simply be, "Thanks Lord." In another entry he wrote, "I believe in personalized self-discipline and self-control. I must think more of and with the God-man." The accomplishments that Ted achieved in the highlands as well as his experience with the Koho people were factors in his deciding to extend his agriculture work to a third year.

Ted sings with his friend, K'Ching

Ted's interest in playing the guitar began from his high school years where he entertained and sang with his friends. He explained, "These folk songs are simply a pleasure and a fun social encounter." In anticipation of such an experience, he took his guitar with him to Vietnam realizing that he may be able to build rapport and friendship with music. He envisioned a place in Di Linh where he and other musicians could come together and share their music. So he and Jeanie began planning for a coffee house, a place where people could come to informally play their music and engage with others. Ted commented on the challenge it would be to have coffee house music engagements. "It's difficult for us to find a time to have such gatherings since the curfew keeps people in their homes in the evening." Once he began to sing songs at a coffee house but the police told him he needed a permit, so he kept searching. Sometimes he engaged the children in music at the nearby Tin Lanh Church. On one occasion he and Jeanie both went downtown where they gave a concert on the sidewalk. When he was in Saigon there was usually a gathering at the VNCS house where he played guitar songs as his colleagues shared in the singing.

Handicrafts

Ted noticed that some of the Montagnard people were skilled artisans and made arts and crafts products which they sold locally. Their creations included baskets, bracelets, pottery, vases, jewelry, fabric, musical instruments and farming tools. He proposed that a larger market in Saigon would be more profitable for them. Therefore, he encouraged them to find a way to transport their products to Saigon. On one occasion when he was going to Saigon for a meeting, he volunteered to take some of their products and search for an outlet. They accepted his offer but it is not known if such a transaction was established in just one attempt but in the passing years, the open air market in Di Linh has grown as well as the sprawling population of the town. Consequently, the opportunity to earn more money from arts and crafts has become more realistic. Di Linh has grown from dirt streets in the 1970s to busy paved streets today.

Physical Conditioning

Ted was self-disciplined in maintaining good physical health. As time permitted, he walked up the hill to the nearby school and played volleyball or engaged children in soccer or throwing the Frisbee. Since he was agile he sometimes did handstands and even walked on his hands, a treat for the Koho school children. He understood the contributions exercise and recreation make toward good health. Accordingly, he was self-motivated to jog as his work allowed. As written in his journal, his running distance was about two miles each time he ran. One of his journal entries at the end of the day was simply, "Thanks for running with me today Lord."

A handstand for his friends at the Koho School

The Di Linh Area

The VNCS house in Di Linh was located on the main street of town (Highway 20). The open-air-market was nearby and the street was constantly busy with traffic mostly consisting of motorbikes, bicycles and a few cars. Vietnam Christian Service volunteers lived in this house from 1966 to 1971 when Ted was killed. Two months later Phyllis Cribby returned to Di Linh where she continued her nursing work from a house a few blocks away from the original VNCS house. Terry Bonnet also lived at the new VNCS location and continued his work in a literacy program. The original house was then converted to other businesses as pictured below. When the war ended in 1975 the VNCS workers throughout the country left Vietnam. In approximately 2007 the house was demolished and the lot was vacant for a few years thereafter. Pictured below is a view of the VNCS house before it was demolished.

Front entrance to the Di Linh VNCS house until late 1971 when it was occupied by other businesses as pictured above.

Side entrance to the VNCS house occupied by other businesses in late 1971

Street level floor

Bottom level floor

Kitchen

Outside porch

Covered porch

Bedroom

Bedroom

Bedroom

Living and
Dining room

| Closet | Shower |
| Closet | Shower |

| Closet | Shower |
| Closet | Shower |

Bedroom

Bedroom

Bathroom

Bathroom

Bath-
room

Front porch

Street

← South to Saigon

North to Dalat →

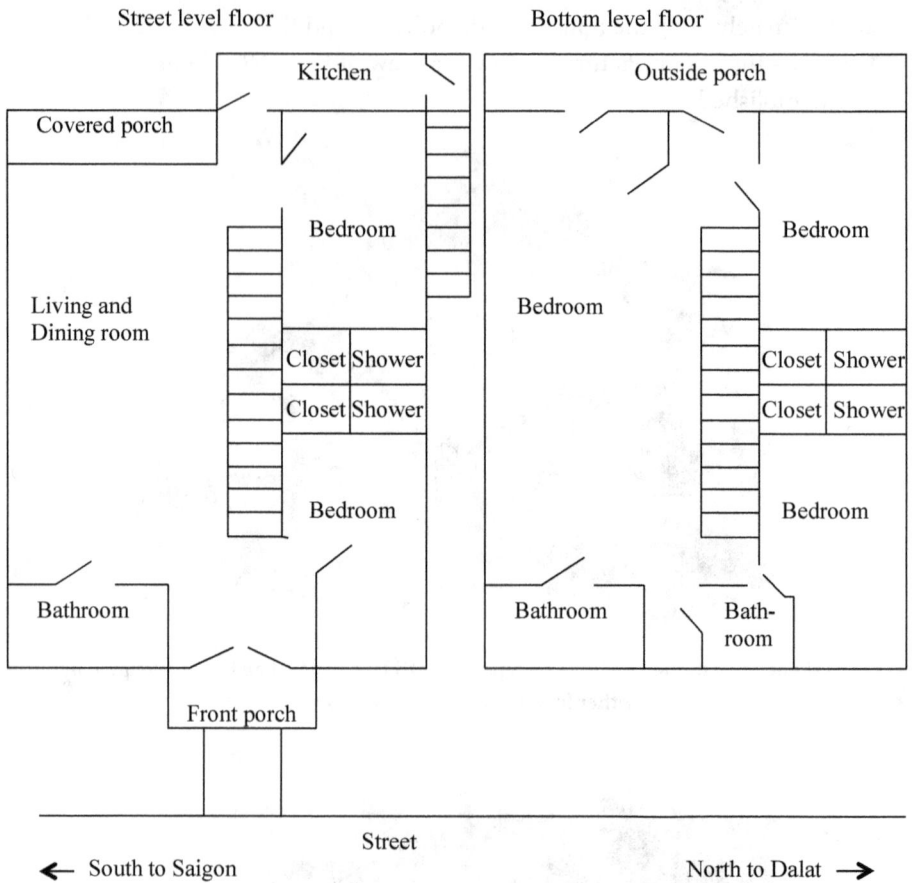

Di Linh VNCS House Floor Plan

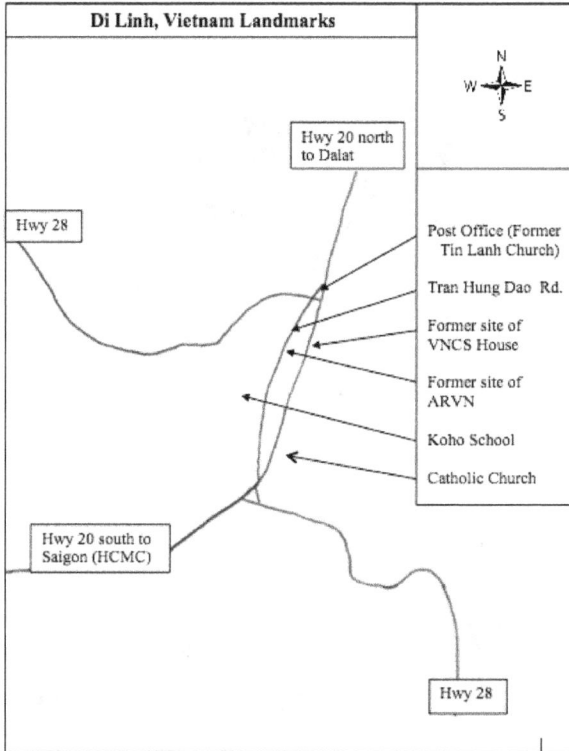

Di Linh, Vietnam (map of business area of town)

K'Krah's daughter and her students

Catholic Church

Koho School

The Di Linh Post Office

Chapter 7

Pakdy

"The purpose of human life is to serve and to show compassion and the will to help others."

—ALBERT SCHWEITZER

WHEN ATTENDING THE TIN Lanh Church in Di Linh (a Christian church), Ted had the thought that he and Pakdy could have their wedding at this church. He was acquainted with the congregation and the pastor. He occasionally played his guitar for the children at this church. He shared this wedding plan secret with Pakdy on one occasion when they were both in Saigon at a VNCS meeting.

About half way through their two years of service Ted and Pakdy agreed to marry but the wedding would not take place until the completion of their two years of work. Ted made it clear to Pakdy that since the wedding would be a long time away it would be necessary to keep the wedding a secret. He knew that once the word got out regarding their marriage the gossip could be a distraction for everyone associated with them. So they both agreed to keep the wedding a secret until closer to the wedding date.

Pakdy and Ted

Shortly after Ted and Pakdy made their agreement Ted received a letter from one of his VNCS colleagues asking when the wedding was going to be. At that point Ted realized that the only way that information could have escaped was by way of Pakdy. As described in Ted's diary, "It's time to lower the boom," meaning, there are some serious questions for Pakdy to answer regarding their secret wedding plans. In a letter written on November 8, 1969, he confronted her with essentially two areas that she needed to address. He decisively told her, "This is not only a matter of you not keeping a secret; it also shows your lack of respect for me." He realized how distressing this letter would be to her and ended his letter by saying he knows she is now in tears and went on to explain that this is not the end, but that this is an area where she needs to consider the consequences of her actions. Additionally he wrote, "Do not come to see me in Di Linh." In his closing remark he assured her of his love before mailing the letter.

When Pakdy received the letter and had time to digest the contents, she immediately went to her supervisor and asked for a leave of absence so she could see Ted. But Mr. Nelson, her supervisor denied the request. In Pakdy's mind, it was an absolute necessity that she see Ted no matter what the consequences. She realized she had not kept a trust and she needed to explain herself and seek Ted's forgiveness. It was absolutely imperative to her that she see Ted in person. Ignoring her supervisor's denial, she went to the bus station and took the seven hour trip to Di Linh. Many apprehensive thoughts were going through her mind during the journey. When she got to the VNCS house Ted was not there but he returned later that day. Their talk began as Pakdy asked for forgiveness. She also explained that an acquaintance kept prying for information about their relationship. Pakdy described the person doing the prodding as a "busy body" who continued until she got the information from Pakdy. As they talked they were able to address some critical issues and come to an understanding as Ted forgave her.

About three months prior to the marriage Ted and Pakdy made a trip to Hong Kong where Pakdy introduced her parents to Ted. They were very happy for their daughter and they gave them their blessing. Pakdy's father then held an engagement party. It was a 10 course Chinese meal served in a nice Chinese restaurant with 22 guests. It was there that Ted presented Pakdy with a diamond ring.

Pakdy had 5 brothers and 2 sisters. The family had fled from the mainland of China to Hong Kong in the early 1950s and some of her family never came out of China. Pakdy was Christianized by missionaries in Hong Kong through the Lutheran Church. She had done child care work in Lutheran nurseries in Hong Kong. She then graduated from college in Taiwan where she majored in Arabic Language. She said it was her desire to study something challenging while in college.

Pakdy's parents and two brothers with Pakdy and Ted

The Wedding

Wedding plans began as the wedding date drew closer. Although Ted requested that his parents not make the trip to Vietnam for the wedding for security reasons he encouraged them and his siblings to participate by sending needed items for the wedding: packets for making punch, food items, decorations, etc.

The very festive Christian wedding was held at the Tin Lanh Church with the Koho minister and Mr. Irwin the Christian Missionary Alliance minister presiding. Pakdy's bridesmaid and the flower girls were friends of the VNCS workers. Ted's best man was his co-worker and friend K'Krah. Music was provided by Koho singers and musicians playing their Koho musical instruments. Pakdy and Ted had designed the announcement and had it printed in English, Koho and Vietnamese. At the bottom of the invitation, Ted wrote a note to his parents and siblings expressing his delight regarding this happy occasion.

The Wedding Party

Ted chose a local girl to be Pakdy's bridesmaid. She was a girl who had a deep affection for Ted but he told her tactfully that he had already chosen Pakdy to be his wife. He then asked her if she would be the bridesmaid which she accepted. Ted wanted to keep the friendship. Accordingly, their friendship remained.

They were married on April 17, 1971. After the wedding and reception they had a delightful visit in the city of Dalat for two days. Upon returning to Di Linh Ted told Pakdy that there was agriculture work he needed to attend to with his co-worker, K'Krah. Pakdy replied, "But it's our honeymoon." Ted responded, "Every day's a honeymoon!"

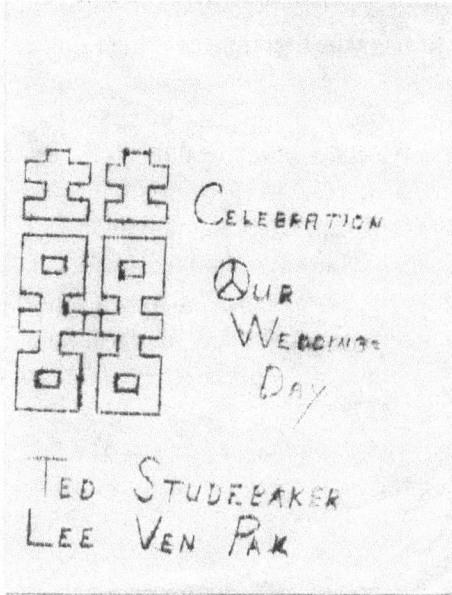

You are cordially invited to attend our wedding which will take place at the Koho Tin Lanh Church in Di Linh, Viet Nam on Saturday, April 17, 1971, at ten o'clock A. M. A celebration party will follow.

Bol hi cho hup ngan nang ja oh mi tus bota tomi au boñ hi di tom Hiu Jum Tin Lanh Kon Cau Djiring Viet Nam ngay 17, konhai poen, 1971, boh jot jo drim. Gos bota konhol mo bota sa tono tombau.

Tran trong kinh moi qui khach vui llong den le nghi hon phoi chung toi o tai Nha Tho Tin Lanh Thuong Di Linh, Viet Nam vao ngay 17, thang tu, 1971, luc muoi gios ang. Du buoi tiec sao khi le.

We'll be married in Koho language and somewhat following the tribal custom, only Christianized. Life is Great! Yea!!

When Pakdy came to Ohio following Ted's death, she lived at the home of Ted's parents in Union, Ohio for about two years as she dealt with the loss of Ted and coped with cultural adjustments, the language and customs in America. She and Ted's mother, Zelma had many talks which Zelma described as a much needed outlet for both of them. Pakdy's relatives sent gracious letters to Ted's parents thanking them for their kindness to Pakdy and expressing their sympathy at Ted's death. They had developed a fond relationship with Ted when they met him for the first time in Hong Kong a few months before the wedding.

Pakdy arrived in the United States with a temporary visa. She expressed a desire to create a new life in America which would call for establishing citizenship. Ted's brother, Lowell accepted the responsibility of helping her seek citizenship and worked with Ohio Representative, Charles Whalen to extend her visa status. Eventually an unlimited extended visa was granted pending future status. In the meantime Lowell managed other business concerns for Pakdy. This included correspondence, medical care, financial concerns, travel arrangements, child care work, Brethren Volunteer Service and college studies.

The first few months of Pakdy's life in America was a period of becoming oriented and deciding how to proceed with her life. It was during this time that Pakdy and Zelma were asked to speak at the Church of the Brethren annual conference where they talked about Ted's commitment to peace and justice. Pakdy made the following presentation.

Dear Friends:

It is a hard time for me to express my feelings. I think most of you already know how I feel about Ted's death but perhaps some of you don't know how much my life was changed since I have known him, especially how he helped me understand more about true love and peace. His simple and humble way of living taught me these things. He expressed his beliefs daily through his work and contacts with others.

Since my life with him was so short, I still don't feel I completely understand all that he did but I think I can continue to learn from his influence and memory and from some of you.

His death was a result of a conflict caused by hate, even though he had demonstrated his own opposition to war. His belief that love is stronger than hate was evident in the way he died. He was truly a man of peace. I'm sure all of you share my grief over his death, but I hope you will grieve more for those who do not understand what he did.

I deeply appreciate the sympathy and comfort that all of you have given to me. I feel especially blessed that Ted and I have such good friends. I believe this is an expression of real Christian love. I hope I will be able to perpetuate Ted's ideas with my life and I want to thank you all for helping to give me strength in this difficult time.

Sincerely,

Pakdy Studebaker

With the help of family and friends, Pakdy continued to see where she might become established with fulfilling pursuits. This included a term of studies at Manchester College, child care work at a church in Dayton, Ohio and serving in Brethren Volunteer Service. Following the BVS training she was assigned to a project in Tucson, Arizona where she assisted in childcare work at the Church of the Brethren child care facility.

After having lived and worked in the United States for eight years, the adjustment remained difficult for Pakdy. Dealing with Ted's death and creating a new life in America presented challenges for her well-being. After much thought and dialogue, it was decided by Pakdy, family and friends that it would be in her best interest to live near her brother who was living near Sydney, Australia. He agreed to assist in establishing his sister near him, so the planning began and the move was eventually made. Ted's brother, Ron worked with Pakdy and her brother to make the transition arrangements and to obtain the flight to Australia. Pakdy then traveled to Australia and established her life near Sydney in close proximity to her brother. In this location she shares a home with her friends and is engaged in Christian activities through her church. She never remarried and has remained in correspondence with friends and Ted's family in the United States.

Chapter 8

The War

"I believe that unarmed truth and unconditional love will have the final word."
—MARTIN LUTHER KING JR.

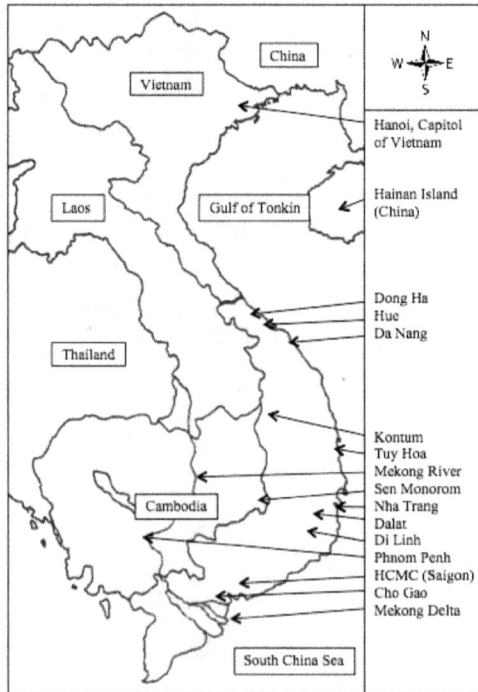

Map of Vietnam

Year	Vietnam Military Timeline
2879 BC to 1945	Vietnam has been invaded by many nations including the Chinese, Japanese, French and Americans. They have also been involved in years of civil war.
1940–1945	Japan controls Vietnam.
1945	Vietnam, Laos and Cambodia are provided with food, clothing and medical supplies by Church World Service due to devastation caused by war.
1946	France resumes fighting for control of Vietnam.
1954	The French were defeated in Vietnam. The Geneva Agreement ruled that Vietnam be divided at the 17th parallel with a Communist government in the north and a democracy in the south.
1954	South Vietnamese President Ngo Dinh Diem begins campaign against political dissidents.
1954	Church World Service began providing assistance to Vietnamese refugees in resettlement areas.
1955	U.S. Military advisors are sent to the war in Vietnam known as "American War" by the Vietnamese. From 1955 to 1975, 58,000 Americans were killed. Estimates for Vietnamese killed range from 600,000 to 1,000,000.
1957	Beginning of Communist insurgency in South Vietnam.
1959–1960	National Liberation Front forms in South Vietnam.
1962	The number of US military advisors in South Vietnam rises to 12,000.
1963	Viet Cong guerrillas operating in South Vietnam, defeat units of the ARVN (the South Vietnamese Army). President Diem is overthrown.
1964	On August 2, 1964 a US destroyer was allegedly attacked by North Vietnamese patrol boats. This triggered the start of pre-planned American bombing raids on North Vietnam.
1965	200,000 American combat troops arrive in South Vietnam.
1966	US troop numbers in Vietnam rise to 400,000, then to 500,000 the following year.
1968	Tet Offensive - An assault by the Viet Cong and the North Vietnamese army on US positions begins. More than 500 civilians die in the US massacre at My Lai.
1969	Ho Chi Minh died. President Nixon begins to reduce US ground troops in Vietnam as domestic public opposition to the war grows.
1970	Nixon's national security advisor, Henry Kissinger, and Le Duc Tho from the Hanoi government, began talks in Paris.

Year	Vietnam Military Timeline
1973	Ceasefire agreement in Paris, US troop pull-out completed by March.
1975	South Vietnamese President Duong Van Minh surrenders. Troops from North Vietnam invade South Vietnam and take control of the entire country.
1976	Socialist Republic of Vietnam proclaimed. Saigon is re-named Ho Chi Minh City. Hundreds of thousands flee abroad including "boat people."
1979	Vietnam invades Cambodia and ousts the Khmer Rouge regime of Pol Pot. In response, Chinese troops cross Vietnam's northern border. They are pushed back by Vietnamese forces. The number of "boat people" trying to leave Vietnam causes international concern.
1989	Vietnamese troops withdraw from Cambodia.
1994	The US lifts its 30-year trade embargo on Vietnam.
2000	US President Bill Clinton pays a three-day official visit to Vietnam. The US pledges more help to clear landmines left over from the war in Vietnam. The Vietnamese government estimates nearly 40,000 people have been killed by unexploded munitions. By 2000, Vietnam had established diplomatic relations with most nations.
2004	The first US commercial flight since the end of the war in Vietnam, lands in Ho Chi Minh City.
2007	Vietnam in cooperation with Japan begins plans for building a high-speed rail link between Hanoi and Ho Chi Minh City. This long term project will begin when funding is available.
2007	The US agrees to help fund a search for ways to remove Agent Orange, the toxic defoliant, from Vietnam.
2011, June	Vietnam begins a joint operation with the United States to clean up contamination from the toxic Agent Orange defoliant widely used by the US military during the war in Vietnam.

IN MANY OF TED'S letters and in frequent diary entries, he referenced the senselessness of the war in Vietnam and called it "a self-perpetuating cycle." After receiving a letter from a hometown politician and seeing what some politicians were saying about the war, Ted realized how out of touch some of our government leaders were and concluded that some were blindly supporting the war solely to advance their political ambitions. He wrote his views to some of them and raised many thought provoking questions to whoever asked him about the war. "What can be done about the war? Why do people have war? I'll never know. It can only be won in the States when people refuse to support the dirty, rotten, inhuman government and the military machine. I'd risk my job here for a good honest peace demonstration. I'm angry at war, corruptness and narrow-mindedness."

In collaboration with his VNCS colleagues in Saigon, Ted described an action they took to oppose the war. "I formally registered my conscientious thoughts of opposition to the US military involvement in Vietnam. Twenty of us signed the paper, presented it to Ambassador Bunker and held a silent vigil in front of the American Embassy." These volunteers realized it's one thing to talk, but actions have a completely different meaning.

One day after a two mile running exercise Ted ended his workout near an ARVN soldier and asked him some questions about the war. "Why the war? Who are the VC? Who is not? Who is telling the truth? Who is not?" The soldier told Ted that he had no answers. Ted realized that the response was representative of the feeling of other soldiers he had talked with. On another day he met and talked with a GI chaplain. "He admits war stinks and says we'll never win and we should not be here in the first place." In reviewing these questions, Ted concluded his diary remarks, "Damned if anybody knows the answers as to why we have a war going on here." His thoughts about bringing the war to an end were echoed by other VNCS colleagues. In one letter Ted stated, "I wish for more moratoriums on the war in the US. That may be the only way to end the war. The politicians talk about an honorable end to it. I can't by any stretch of reason, see how the US can ever hope for an honorable end to a dishonorable, illegal and immoral war that it is fully responsible for starting." Ted continued, "The sight of the US government in Vietnam continually scalds me. How could the US be so damn stupid?" While writing a letter to his family back home he said, "If you want to help me, tell the people to write a letter to their congressman in Washington D.C. including everybody in the church. They need to be voicing their opinions about this war now!"

The blunders left behind by the war were beyond comprehension and continually before Ted. Upon reading about the My Lai Massacre, he criticized "the sickening tactics of war. When will they ever learn? What can I do with my body and mouth? The war and U.S. aid is the real blame."

When Ted heard about the actions of a peace activist from his home area, he wrote home with his comments of support:

> It's encouraging to hear about people who are still trying to bring about social justice through humanistic concern in an active and

committed way. One only has to read Newsweek, Time or Life about the My Lai incident to grasp some understanding of the unnecessary, illegal and immoral actions the US government is committing in Vietnam. I have tried hard to find some small reason for US involvement in this war but my search has only seemed to unveil the opposite, that it is the National Liberation Front (NLF) who actually has a reason to fight. The US government has got to be the biggest and worst liar. I realize you all know the terribleness of war and what it does, but no one can begin to really understand what it's like for the Vietnamese and Montagnard people of Vietnam. I guess I just need to release some of the frustration I have. I hope that something can be done to stop the war. I've often wondered whether I wouldn't have served a higher calling had I held a sign in a demonstration in front of the Pentagon for two years instead of being another American clogging up Vietnam and adding more fuel to the huge corruption furnace that consumes everything and affects everybody over here. The truth is all war is hell and by a little common sense we should all be able to see that war, especially this one is self-perpetuating. I really believe the US government, military and corrupt aid has caused the very opposition we are now at war with.

Ted experienced being the ugly, rich American when he traveled in Vietnam and concluded that

"I have a better look at what the American war economy has had on the general population and it isn't a success story for the red, white and blue, that's for certain." While driving to the nearby village of Boa Loc, Ted counted the bodies of eleven VC that lay along the road. "I think again about the future but not too much time for that stuff. I hope I live to see the end of war and I hope it's soon." On another occasion, a woman told Ted her husband was taken to Boa Loc and jailed because he was suspected of giving food to the VC. "War is hell, hell, hell and people are frightened. Talk is that the VC will attack again tonight for the 3rd night straight. Here's hoping my life holds out Lord along with other people who think as T. Wayne does, Life is Great, Yea."

The VNCS staff in Di Linh were aware of the procedures for taking cover in the closet bunker beneath the stair steps. In a letter to Pakdy, Ted described one of these battles. "Last night was the 2nd night in a row the VC attacked Di Linh. The first night the VC killed 23 soldiers on the hill above our house and twice as many were wounded. What a hellish mess. I saw flesh, bone, blood and the dead. The non-rationality of war is now real to me." In a follow up letter to Pakdy he described another horrific scene near the VNCS house.

> Last night there was a VC mortar attack on Di Linh and 5 or 6 people were killed. This time the mortars did not land so close to our house but some of the dead were civilians and relatives of some friends of ours. Terry and I tried to help by taking the bodies by truck to a nearby village so the relatives could mourn their death. This is a Montagnard custom. It was a sickening experience for me to help with the washing and cleaning of two of the dead boys only 12 and 16 years old. This experience only makes me more disgusted and angry at all people (American, VC, Vietnamese or anyone) who participates in the process of war. Fighting and war is senseless today. It has no meaning; it does not assure peace but only more war.

It was for these security reasons that Ted discouraged Pakdy from visiting him in Di Linh.

The headquarters for the MACV in Di Linh was across the street (Route 20) from the VNCS house. The MACV location was at the top of a hill about 200 yards from the VNCS house. It was here that several American helicopter gunships landed each day transporting supplies and troops. On some occasions as many as 160 GIs were brought there. With an influx of troops there was increased prostitution, black markets, higher prices and displaced people. In a letter to Pakdy, Ted described these side effects of war.

> How cruel and unnecessary. Where is humanistic concern? Where is humility and honesty when you see the burning of fields and homes? I sometimes feel that Vietnam does not need me but only peace so that people can live without refugee camps, relief goods, military men and equipment everywhere. I really believe that my work in Vietnam is really much more beneficial to me than the people I am trying to help. I have seen and experienced a lot of good and bad about development and social work here in Vietnam. This is an education.

In their exchange of letters, Ted and Pakdy described some of the difficulties of working in a country during a war. They agreed to talk about these challenges when they could talk in person. Ted's letters often contained words of encouragement to Pakdy. He closed one of his letters with the following comment. "Work here is sometimes very difficult for me but I must remember God requires effort, not success, right?"

The website at http://civilianpublicservice.org by the Mennonite Central Committee, contains a video with a narrative as told by Paul Leatherman at the time he was director of Vietnam Christian Service from 1966 to 1968. His story comprises the characteristics and commitment of many individuals who engage in nonviolent work for peace and justice. The program used US government surplus to feed 50,000 children each day who were placed in refugee camps as a result of the war. American government officials became very concerned about this and one day the American ambassador, Ellsworth Bunker came to visit Paul. The following is their dialogue:

"Mr. Leatherman, I understand you are operating hospitals here in Vietnam, is that correct?" "Yes, we have a hospital in Nah Trang and Pleiku." The ambassador then asked, "Are you treating the Viet Cong?" Mr. Leather responded, "Mr. Ambassador, we don't look at anybody's ID card, we don't care who they are. If someone is sick and they need hospitalization, we'll take care of them. If a wounded person shows up and they need treatment, we'll take care of them. We don't ask who they are or what their political persuasion is." The ambassador then asked, "I understand you are feeding a lot of refugee children, is this correct?" Mr. Leatherman answered, "Absolutely." The ambassador next asked, "Are these children of the Viet Cong?" The response was the same, "Mr. Ambassador, again, we do not ask what their political persuasion is, we don't care, that's not a concern of ours." The ambassador replied, "Mr. Leatherman, if you are treating the Viet Cong in your hospitals, that's treason and do you know the penalty for treason?" Mr. Leatherman continued, realizing that the Holy Spirit had given him a confident response, "Mr. Bunker, I'm here with Vietnam Christian Service representing the church. We have a book that you may or may not know that tells us that we should feed the hungry, treat the wounded and sick, that we should cloth the naked and if we don't do that, I know the penalty for that and we're going to keep doing what we're doing.

On that comment the meeting was ended, the ambassador departed and the subject never came up again."

Unintended Consequences of War

Ted described some of the many unintended and painful consequences that resulted from the war in Vietnam. He proclaimed to all who would listen that the decision makers who involved men and women in this war were immoral. In a letter he wrote home with pressing urgency, he stated, "If you want to help me, tell the people to write a letter to their congressman in Washington D.C. including everybody in the church. They need to be voicing their opinions about this war now!"

In his diary and letters, Ted described some of the many "devastating, demoralizing and dehumanizing effects of the war:"

- The death of innocent victims including children
- Suffering
- Destruction
- The increase of refugees and the resulting need for housing, health care and education
- Prostitution
- Drug abuse
- The spread of crime
- Increased prison population and the resulting difficulties
- Family problems
- Hatred and misunderstanding between warring nations exist for generations
- Corruption

Max Ediger, in his book, "Friendships of Gold," explained the image of horror that remained etched in a soldier's memory for the rest of his life when he realized the grenade he had just thrown had killed an innocent young girl who had smiled at him a moment after he had thrown the hand grenade.

In one of Ted's letters, he described an incident where an American soldier walked into the Di Linh VNCS house uninvited, a disregard for entering private property. Upon seeing Ted, the soldier informed him that he was looking for prostitutes.

Americans who have served in a country devastated by war and poverty, sometimes choose to spend their lives providing requested services to the people of such a country. They are aware of the fulfillment that comes by finding ways to contribute toward the livelihood and economic progress of the country and their help is gratefully accepted. After working through VNCS, Bill Herod chose to live in Cambodia to promote the preservation of the Bunong hill tribe culture in the town of Sen Monorom in the eastern highland region of Cambodia.

The following paper written by Bill Herod describes the disconnect between "American intentions (winning hearts and minds, nation building, democracy, equality, freedom, etc.) and the realities faced by American troops on the ground who are placed in an impossible situation."

How the War in Afghanistan is Like the War in Vietnam

1. The reality for US troops is bewilderment, fear, frustration and destruction. Their job becomes perplexing. Who or where is the enemy? How to function in local society? What is the point of this military exercise? Take a hill? Secure a road? Blow up a village? Why? How will that advance the cause? What is the cause? As was true in Vietnam, American troops are our representatives in Afghanistan. They are the Americans the people actually see and with whom they may have some interaction. It is the presence and conduct of our troops, not our policies or policy makers to which local people react. Also, as was true in Vietnam, American troops are victims in Afghanistan. We have sent them to do the impossible and they must pay the price personally in many ways.

2. In Vietnam, it was tunnels and jungles. In Afghanistan, it is caves and mountain passes. Locals know the area and live and move easily in the countryside ("like fish in water"). Americans are exposed, relatively stationary and dependent on massive supply networks for everything from soup to socks. To the Americans, the terrain and climate are inhospitable and debilitating. To the locals, Vietnamese or Afghanis, this is home.

3. As in Vietnam, the Afghanis who resist us are fighting for their lives, their way of life, their families and their land. They have nowhere to go. Defeat or surrender are unthinkable. Withdrawal is not an option. To fight the invaders is a sacred and patriotic duty. Death on the battlefield is martyrdom. Not to fight the invaders is treason and cowardice.

   In the 60's in Vietnam I saw fields of bodies of fallen revolutionary soldiers cut down by U.S. "dragon fire" that put a bullet every four inches across the whole area. Those incredibly brave young warriors never had a chance against the massive U.S. firepower thrown at them. At the time I thought they were foolish, misguided, their action hopeless and futile. Then I realized that Vietnamese students I knew were leaving school to replace those whose riddled bodies we had seen in the fields, their brothers, uncles, and friends.

In the 80's I walked through well-tended martyrs' cemeteries throughout Vietnam where hundreds of thousands of such young people are buried and honored for their heroic and victorious resistance to American occupation.

4. American soldiers can't tell the "good guys from the bad guys." Troops either assume all locals are potential enemies and treat them as such or they assume all locals are harmless and then are easily tricked, trapped or ambushed. Either way, damage is done to the image of the Americans, to the psychological well-being of the troops themselves and to the local people they encounter.

5. American forces on the ground are completely out of their element and have little information about or respect for local culture. They make inappropriate comments and gestures toward women, children, elders, shop keepers, religious symbols or practices, etc., with profound impact on the way local people think of them and, by extension, their "cause" whatever it is perceived to be. Their presence endangers the lives of local people they employ or befriend who are marked for life as lackeys or traitors. We saw this in Vietnam and we are seeing it in Afghanistan.

6. There was a disproportionate response using the sledgehammer to swat the mosquito in Vietnam. There were many stories of "destroying the village in order to save it." In Afghanistan there are accounts of bombing wedding parties or incinerating a mountainside where villagers were thought to be retrieving bodies of fallen family members, etc.

7. The Americans are seen as corrupt, corrupting and corruptible. Wartime Saigon's black market was famous for its variety of U.S. military equipment: weapons, ammunition, medicines, field gear, bright orange "U.S. Mail" bags, etc. I was once offered a new Lotus helicopter, un-assembled, in crates for $1,500. In Afghanistan, the U.S. provides the market for the huge flow of drugs supporting both "our" warlords and the Taliban. As in Vietnam, Afghan elections are manipulated; aid money is squandered and a new class of super-rich is created and coddled.

8. The attempt to impose our will and our values on people with a different culture, religion, experience, hopes and dreams is doomed. Worse, this attempt is counterproductive when local people see American troops as undisciplined thugs or marauding infidels. In Afghanistan, American actions generate or intensify resistance to our occupation as was the case in Vietnam.

9. The Americans think of military operations in terms of months or years. The people of Vietnam and Afghanistan think in terms of decades, generations or centuries. Both have long and proud histories of repelling invading armies from powerful countries no matter how long it takes or how great the cost.

10. In both Saigon and Kabul we inserted our chosen leaders, attempted to prop them up with money and weapons and hoped they would somehow become "legitimate." They didn't.

Ted stated in his writings, "One thing is for certain I will not be a part of the senseless killing that occurs in war." Through his courses and reading, he had studied the lives of nonviolent peace and justice leaders as listed in the timeline below:

Martyr/Date	Selected Nonviolent Peace Leaders
Jesus Christ BC — 30 to 33 AD Crucified and arose	Jesus Christ is the central figure of Christianity. He taught followers to love their enemies and to return good for evil.
Dirk Willems 1500s–1569	Dirk Willems was a Dutch Anabaptist who was imprisoned for his Anabaptist beliefs. He escaped from prison by safely crossing over the moat of thin ice due to his light weight from eating prison rations. His pursuer however had fallen through the ice while chasing Willems and called for help. Willems turned back to save the life of his pursuer. He was recaptured, tortured and killed for his faith.
John Kline 1797–1864	John Kline was a German Baptist Brethren minister who traveled an estimated 100,000 miles on horseback to West Virginia and beyond visiting Brethren families, preaching, baptizing and establishing churches. He also learned herbal medicine and treated the sick using herbs that he gathered. During the Civil War, he obtained permission from officers in the Northern and Southern armies to cross military lines on horseback to visit Brethren families in the North and South. He also corresponded with the Governor of Virginia and other officials on behalf of Brethren and Mennonite men who were opposed to serving in the military. At one point, he was arrested and jailed for his opposition to the war and his support of Anabaptists who opposed it. He also spoke out against slavery. In 1864 as he was returning home from a meeting at the Nettle Creek Church in Indiana, he was shot and killed by ardent confederates. Although he was aware of the dangers that surrounded him, he steadfastly followed his calling to serve his Lord and his church.

Martyr/Date	Selected Nonviolent Peace Leaders
Seth Laughlin 1800s–1864	Seth was living in Virginia with his wife and 7 children during the Civil War. He wasn't raised in the Quaker faith, but converted in adulthood. Seth was arrested, tortured, and eventually died in prison because of his refusal to kill another human being.
Mahatma Gandhi 1883–1944	Through the use of nonviolent resistance in South Africa and India, Gandhi led nationwide campaigns for easing poverty, expanding women's rights, building religious and ethnic amity. He was assassinated in 1948 on his way to address a prayer meeting.
Clayton Kratz 1896–1920	In 1920 Clayton Kratz was traveling with two other MCC friends to the war-torn and famine-stricken Russian Mennonites in Ukraine. Their mission was to investigate their needs and to bring relief. Within two months of their arrival, Clayton was arrested and vanished.
Dietrich Bonhoeffer 1906–1945	Bonhoeffer was a German, Lutheran pastor who was hanged at the age of 39 for opposing Adolph Hitler. He was outspoken about Nazi dictatorship and Hitler's persecution of the Jews. He became sensitive to social injustices experienced by minorities and was troubled by the weakness of the church to effectively address this issue. Bonhoeffer was resolved to carry out the teachings of Christ as revealed in the Gospels. He was a pacifist, but when he realized the atrocities that were taking place he saw the need to oppose the Hitler regime. He then became involved in a plot to overthrow Adolf Hitler which led to his imprisonment and execution.
Martin Luther King Jr. 1929–1968	King was an American Baptist minister, activist, humanitarian, and leader in the African-American Civil Rights Movement. He advanced civil rights using nonviolent civil disobedience based on his Christian beliefs. He led boycotts and nonviolent protests and helped organize the 1963 March on Washington where he delivered the historic, "I Have a Dream" speech. He spoke out against the war in Vietnam and the need to address poverty and jobs. He also won the Noble Peace Prize. In 1968 he was fatally shot in Memphis, Tennessee.

Chapter 9

Correspondence

"I am firmly of the belief that he who takes a stand is occasionally and even often wrong, but he who never takes a stand is always wrong."

—TED STUDEBAKER

SOMETIMES TED EXPRESSED HIS views regarding the implications of the war to the news media and people in leadership positions. He wrote about his disgust with government authorities whose meaningless decisions led to the devastating consequences that he saw first-hand. When he challenged the news media's coverage of the war, some wrote back by challenging his views, others responded by justifying their news coverage while others chose to simply not take a stand at all, but his challenges undoubtedly prompted them to reconsider their journalism accuracy.

Confronting Apathy

Ted used one of his vacation leaves to attend the International Conference on Social Welfare in Manila. While he was there, he visited the Rice Research Institute so he could be more effective in his agriculture work. He was grateful to be in Manila where he experienced the differences from Di Linh. He noticed how liberating it was to have no curfews, reasonable prices, hot water showers and no sounds of artillery at night. Ice cream and soda were another treat. After the conference he composed and sent a letter in response to one of the speakers:

October 4, 1970
Di Linh, Vietnam

Dear Dr. Schottland,

I feel compelled to express my thoughts on a subject which I believe should have had a high priority at the recent Institute for Clinical Social Work (ICSW) which I attended in Manila but which unfortunately was hardly ever mentioned. I am referring to the wasteful and inhumane process of war. I can think of no other human action which has had and continues to have such a devastating, demoralizing and dehumanizing effect on such a large number of innocent people. I was disgusted that people so involved in and so concerned about international social welfare could attend and leave a conference such as the 15th ICSW without facing and acting upon the realities of wars which are presently raging in our world.

I was disappointed that your opening speech did not include as one of your six priorities for social welfare, the immediate end to the destruction, corruption, social disorganization and needless suffering which accompanies war. I felt almost as if no one really wanted to "rock the boat" or interfere with the pious like politeness of the conference in order to dig into one of the biggest problems of world welfare; war.

If, as you hurriedly stated that the ICSW has "cried out against poverty, ill health, war . . . ," why did I not hear those cries against war at the Manila conference? Even the well-prepared and lengthy Report of the Pre-Conference Working Party made no mention of war. The only mention I found relating to world peace and the cry against war is this watered-down, meaningless statement, "Basic to the social well-being of mankind should be the achievement of world peace." Certainly no rational person, no matter what his political background, would disagree with that statement.

I believe that the ICSW not only could have done something in the way of positive and influential action, but has the responsibility to act and to cry out loud, clear and unashamedly against the war in Southeast Asia and the Middle East war. As the National Welfare Rights Organization advocates, governments must change their priorities from an emphasis on death and destruction to an emphasis on life and peace.

As a form of positive social action, I suggest that a committee be formed to prepare a statement after research and discussion, which would be presented and discussed at the next ICSW for adoption. Further, that such a statement be sent to governments of those nations actively involved in the process of war, destruction and the arms race. In short, I feel that the ICSW should back up its words with actions.

I would appreciate knowing your comments and suggestions for positive action on this matter.

Sincerely,

Ted Studebaker
Volunteer agriculturalist
Di Linh, Vietnam

A Letter to Time Magazine

In early April of 1971, after reading an article about the war in Vietnam which had spread across the border to Laos, Ted wrote a letter to Time, the weekly magazine, in response to their news report. Taking time out of his already busy schedule, he felt this issue was too urgent to simply ignore. His letter expressed his outrage at such an immoral action.

Time and Life Building
Rockefeller Center
New York, N.Y. 10020

I was disgusted to read your reports on the Laos invasion. How can you devote complete coverage to the statistical body count type of military analysis and completely ignore any mention as to what might be the fate of the civilians who were once living in those areas now reshaped by 30,000 bombs, rockets and artillery fire. The military assumption is simple, they were all "enemy" if they were unlucky enough to live in the area, every man, woman and baby. So the body counts rise, the war machine rolls on and Tricia's wedding plans rate more concern than the fate of thousands of civilian human beings in Laos.

Ted Studebaker
Vietnam Christian Service
Di Linh, Lam Dong

This time Ted received a response as follows:

Dear Mr. Studebaker,

We respect your compassion for the people of Laos and we share it. There was not a great deal that we could say however in our coverage of the invasion about the future of these people, which is speculative at best. Our concern was given to the facts of the invasion as it progressed, a function of a news magazine. We will continue of course to cover Indochina and to have stories on how refugees are being taken care of and their life, just as we have in the past on the people of Vietnam.

We send best wishes to you in your work in Vietnam.

Sincerely,

Barbara Storfer

The response from Time Magazine did not address Ted's concerns, yet it was a reply. Ted simply sought to present his case, to prompt some thinking and to not allow a journalism publication to go unchallenged. His purpose was to make known an obvious truth that was ignored by Time Magazine.

Corresponding with friends and relatives gave Ted a welcome opportunity to update and share with them. Here is one such letter:

May 11, 1970
Di Lin, Vietnam

Dear Verda Mae and Harry (aunt and uncle),

Greetings to you and family,

From the news, I read there was a recent student protest on the OSU campus. Protests and student demonstrations seem inevitable as long as present government policies remain as they are. Thank goodness at least there are some students who refuse to allow present conditions to remain unchanged and unchallenged.

My work here in agriculture keeps me busy. I recently purchased a dandy rice huller and polisher which I power with a 12 horsepower diesel engine off of one of our rototillers. This huller-polisher machine really does a fine job and should be a real asset to the Montagnard farmers in the area. They have always done the job with mortar and pestle.

You should see their expression when they see that white rice rolling out of the polisher so quick and easy. I hope this will prompt them to raise more rice to sell for a profit. Fifty kilos of white rice here is worth 2000 piasters (about $18.00 U.S. dollars). Typically the Montagnard only raises enough rice for his family to use for one season. There is little or no profit motive, but they are learning!

Best wishes to everyone.

Peace,

Ted

A Letter to the Home Church

On May 31, 1970 Ted wrote a letter to his home Church. There was an urgency to share his observations about how the war is making it difficult for the Koho people to make a living and conduct a normal life when the war continues to bring destruction on a daily basis. This is the letter he wrote:

From: Ted Studebaker

Date: May 31, 1970

Subject: An Open Letter to the Church

Dear Friends,

I find it difficult to write this letter, realizing that while I want to be congenial and informative, I also feel the need to express realistically some of my frustrations and thoughts concerning my present situation.

Please know that I feel most fortunate to work here in Vietnam as a volunteer agriculturalist for Vietnam Christian Service. Some of the most challenging, educational and highly disgusting moments of my life have been experienced during my short one year of work with the Koho tribe of Montagnards here in the highlands of Vietnam. Other than to say that my work is in agriculture, I will not go into detail about specific projects. For those who are interested, I have enclosed some reports and literature describing my work, projects and some material concerning the political-military situation as seen from inside Vietnam.

Second only to my family, you as representatives of the West Milton Church of the Brethren are responsible for my thoughts and actions concerning conscientious objection to the military, my pacifistic views and my voluntary service. Without the church, as skeptical as I am about it now, I might find myself in a uniform as part of a giant military machine whose reason for existence seems based on economics and a big myth. The meaninglessness, the wastefulness and non-necessity of this war is outweighed only by its inhumane effects, both here and in the States. It is beyond my capability to understand how rational people can continue to follow and support (either knowingly or unknowingly, directly or indirectly) the policies of President Nixon and his military advisors.

But like Tim Reiman says, "Let me dissent from despair," for there is hope among the students and humanists who refuse to let these injustices and atrocities go uncontended. May their voices, symbolizing commitment to the fight for justice and morality and their flowers and marshmallows, symbolizing the power of love and nonviolence continue and grow.

I have an idea that most of you who hear these words are sympathetic to my thoughts and feelings. However, it saddens me to know, as beautiful as are all your intentions that you are probably doing considerably more to further US military and imperialistic policy here through the taxes you continue to pay every year, than you are toward the cause of peace and reconciliation. Since being here, I have come to see and realize the tremendous influence of the American military and USAID money that is literally poured into this corrupt country and government. The longer I am here and as my language ability improves, I begin to see more of the complexities of the situation. I do not pretend to understand all of the whys and wherefores of this crisis, but one thing stands out clear in my mind. THIS WAR IS IMMORAL AND WRONG, AND THE BURDEN OF BLAME IS UPON THE US MILITARY, THE US GOVERNMENT, AND THE US PEOPLE. I believe there is a lot of truth in the statement that the killing and destruction will stop only when American public opinion demands it. I recall the words of a great contemporary thinker and activist, Eldridge Cleaver, "Oh judgment, thou art fled to brutish beasts and men have lost their reason."

These are the thoughts that are heavy on my mind right now that I feel the necessity to share with you. It is my hope that reason will once again be restored in the hearts and minds of reasonable men and women.

I express my appreciation to those who have shown interest in my struggles and joys here in Vietnam. Please know that I am in good health and adequate security. I would welcome your responses and comments and will do my best to respond to personal letters if you have questions.

I send my best wishes and regards to all.

Working for Peace,

Ted Studebaker

Volunteer Agriculturalist

Vietnam Christian Service

Di Linh, Vietnam

Ted's letter to his home church (above) was printed in a local newspaper near Ted's home town. A man and his wife who had read the article wrote to Ted expressing their objection to his position on the war. In telling Ted of their disappointment with his letter, they questioned if Vietnam Christian Service was indeed a Christian organization. They further stated that Communist propaganda had influenced Ted. The letter went on to cite a chapter in the Bible about honoring the government.

They wrote that it is ridiculous to view the war as immoral; that many who use these words are themselves immoral in character. After further words of rebuke, the letter finally admonished Ted to get his views straight and study the word of God and this will help him in his Christian life. The couple stated that Americans have high regard for human life and the ideals of Communism do not respect human beings. They closed by stating the reasons why we must become involved in war.

Ted had addressed these same issues before coming to Vietnam in his discussions, written papers and presentations. On April 25, 1971 he wrote the following letter in response then shared his letter with his trusted VNCS co-worker Phyllis Cribby for her evaluation and thoughts. Phyllis told him she thought the letter was an honest and thoughtful response to the realities that were happening in Vietnam. She fully concurred with Ted's response.

Response to Criticism

April 25, 1971

Dear Mr. and Mrs. Peters,

I want to thank you for taking the time to write to me concerning the letter I wrote to my church some months back, which was printed in the Troy Newspaper last March. Even though our views and beliefs seem very far apart concerning war, peace and Christian responsibility, I see this as a great opportunity for me to better understand how "Devout Christians," as you both must be, feel about this very important issue of our country's involvement here in Vietnam and S.E. Asia.

Please know that I have read and reread your letter several times, and shared it with friends working here. I feel it would be worthless for me to continue any debate by letter, since both our views seem to be unswayable, and a letter is no way to discuss such great issues.

Just one point I want to make clear to you. I do not feel the enemy is "right" any more than I feel the US military is "right" here. I believe strongly in trying to follow the example of Jesus Christ as best I know how. Above all, Christ taught me to love all people, including enemies, and to return good for evil, and that all men are brothers in Christ. I condemn all war and conscientiously refuse to take part in it in any active or violent way. I believe that love is a stronger and more enduring power than hatred for my fellow man, regardless of who they are or what they believe.

You probably think I'm pretty idealistic and by your letter, indicate that I'm a pretty mixed up kid. But, I can't apologize for any part of the letter I wrote to my church, since it well represents honestly and sincerely my feelings and concerns about this particular situation. I have tried to speak from both experience and reason, not from mere emotion or hearsay.

I do appreciate your letter for reasons you'll probably never know Mr. and Mrs. Peters. I hope that reason, understanding, and wisdom will guide our thoughts and actions in whatever we think or do. Thank you for inquiring about my safety. Please know that I am in excellent health and adequate security. I know that I am a fortunate man and life is great to me.

Sincerely,

Ted Studebaker
VNCS, Volunteer Agriculturalist
Di Linh, Vietnam

The respect with which this letter was written is noted in Ted's response. His critic provided an open door for Ted to once again express himself regarding the consequences of the war and his beliefs. He furthermore knew that his security was not in this world. He also knew what God requires of each individual as he had had previously stated, "A man's life should be properly balanced and firmly set upon the solid foundation of the individual's belief in and relationship to God."

He well understood that working for peace and justice through alternative service would not be viewed by the majority of society as a rational use of one's time and energy. This, of course would not sway him to remain silent in the face of the devastating consequences of the war. It was the letter from this critic that provided the stage for Ted to once again simply state his views. Minutes after Ted had written this letter and asked Phyllis to review it with him, he was killed when the invaders lodged a barrage of explosives at the back door of the VNCS house where they entered. Throughout the tragic events that followed, Phyllis was mindful of the important document that Ted had written and kept it protected by making copies of it and taking it to his parents.

Chapter 10

Pilgrimage to Di Linh

"We must be ready to allow ourselves to be interrupted by God. God will
constantly be crossing our paths and canceling our plans."

—DIETRICH BONHOEFFER

DURING THE YEARS FOLLOWING Ted's death, several persons have visited
Vietnam and included the town of Di Linh in their itinerary. This included
the following:

- Former Vietnam Christian Service volunteers who had worked in Di
  Linh
- A group of college students, associates and professors
- Relatives of Ted.

Jerry and Judy Aaker (VNCS volunteers in Di Linh)

In 1966, Jerry and Judy Aaker were the first Vietnam Christian Service volunteers to serve in Di Linh, Vietnam. Jerry was a social worker and Judy
was a nurse. They were asked to start a new program that served the many
needs of Koho refugees who were displaced by the war. They were joined
by two other VNCS workers, Betty Theissen, a Mennonite nurse and Lee
Brumback, a Lutheran Agriculturalist. Jerry and Judy returned to Vietnam
on November 24, 1998 with their son Brett, to visit Di Linh and other sites

in Vietnam. Jerry described this return visit in his book, "A Spirituality of Service," a very thought provoking book where Jerry reflects on a life-long journey of faith and work among the world's poor.

Judy and Brett, our son have joined me in Vietnam as part of our commitment to bring Bret back to the place of his birth, as well as for us to see places of great emotional significance from our past. On this day we traveled from Ho Chi Minh City to approximately 150 miles north to Di Linh along the central highway, a route we had never taken during our years in Vietnam. Dr. Loc insisted on being our guide and interpreter, for which we were very appreciative. As we approached Di Linh, we were astounded by the changes in the landscape. Land once sprinkled with a few tea plantations on the hillsides and rice paddies in the valleys was now completely taken over by coffee plantations. Upon entering the town, we were initially disoriented. The outdoor market was not where it had been, the two Tin Lanh Churches were gone, and the hospital where Judy worked was now a school of some sort. I walked past the little building that had served as a morgue at that time and I remembered back to a tragic day in 1967 when the outskirts of our town had been attacked by a unit of the North Vietnamese Army. The next day I stood here looking on in dismay as a truckload of bodies, 30 or 40 Montagnard (tribal) soldiers were loaded to a chorus of loudly sobbing wives, children and mothers.

We decided to go to the office of the Catholic Church to ask a few questions and get some orientation. There we were welcomed by two priests, one of whom we vaguely recognized. With reason: he was Fr. Quang, who has been serving as a priest in Di Linh since 1954! Fr. Quang said he remembered the work of our organization during the war. He said, "I have your secretary right here," and he went to the next room to call him. Out came K'Krah, who as a young man had worked with us as an assistant and interpreter, not a secretary. I recognized him immediately; thin and slightly hunched, his bronze face was now etched with a few wrinkles. But it was his gentle smile that brought back memories of the mild demeanor that marked his character. This was one of those heart-stopping moments. What a delight and surprise for all of us!

We walked down the street to our old house, and K'Krah introduced us to the current occupants who run a restaurant and a hostel there now. We were like kids in a candy shop showing Brett the place we lived before he was born. We looked into some of the rooms but did not go into the one room that had been our bedroom. That was where Ted Studebaker, one of our successors, was killed in 1971. We've heard two versions of what happened that awful night. What is quite certain is that this is one of those terrible mistakes that happen in war, not a planned attack by the local Viet Cong or NVA soldiers. It is clear from many accounts that Ted was much loved by local Vietnamese and Koho people. Ted was a conscientious objector from the Church of the Brethren, serving as a volunteer and had recently married a young Chinese woman. K'Krah said he was there on the night Ted was killed. "I carried his body out of the room," he said with an emotion that he clearly could not articulate well to us in English.

K'Krah proudly introduced us to his family, a beautiful wife, his daughter and her husband and baby. We carefully took down all the names of K'Krah's eight children, took pictures and promised to try to communicate. But in his situation, we found out later, postal service is either nonexistent or the letter that we sent later from Ho Chi Minh City was intercepted. We never heard back from him.

As we left Di Linh, many thoughts circulated in my head. What about the many years of missionary work our neighbors, George and Harriet Irwin invested to build up the two Tin Lanh Churches that are now torn down, one for Vietnamese and the other for a vibrant tribal community? Was it worth the effort? They spent essentially their lives in Vietnam, spoke Vietnamese, Koho and French and lived close to the people. What happens to the Church, the Body of Christ, when it suffers? Living through years of war, violence, political turmoil, repression and fear, the organized church has endured much. The buildings were gone, but I trust not all the followers. I asked K'Krah, "What did you do when the government changed?" He said, "I was a smart man, I went to the mountains with my family to live for several years." Eventually he came back and dedicated his life to Christ through work with the church.

I gave thanks for those of good will and their ministry of presence and prayed for K'Krah, his family and his continuing witness; for the churches, Catholic and Tin Lanh; for missionaries and Vietnamese pastors, that their witness of the past will bear fruit even today, for the ped-cab drivers who were in the south Vietnamese military and are now ostracized for having fought on the wrong side; for government leaders that they might see and know the importance of reconciliation and respect for the sacrifices of all.

Jerry and Judy Aaker
August 20, 2016

Jean C Lindsey (VNCS volunteer in Di Linh)

Jean was the VNCS nurse when Ted arrived in Di Linh in the summer of 1969. Ted appreciated Jean's suggestions and was grateful for her support as he sought ways to make wise use of his time in Di Linh. Jean was a respected colleague and Ted valued sharing ideas with her.

Jean described her visit to Di Linh when she returned with her husband, Jack Lindsay:

> We visited Di Linh in January of 2013. We made two trips from Dalat to Di Linh to see K'Lai and K'Krah. We stopped at the Honda dealership in Di Linh and had a brief visit with Mr. Lai and Mr. Thu. They were both at the Honda dealership, and they were very warm and welcoming. Unfortunately, I do not have a clear memory of these two men but that was also 44 years prior to our visit.
>
> The reunions with K'Lai and K'Krah and their families were amazing. The warmth and hospitality were very wonderful and it was very apparent that they had prepared for our visits. I first spoke with K'Lai from the airport in Dalat, and he said that he thought that we had probably forgotten him. I told him "no way" that he and K'Krah had been in our hearts and minds ever since leaving Di Linh. How could we ever forget them? What a warm and trusting relationship we all had with K'Lai and K'Krah. K'Lai was always a little more playful and outgoing, K'Krah a little more serious and hard-working. Yet he too could get a twinkle in his eye, and we loved and relied on both of them all of the time.
>
> It was heartbreaking to learn from Gary and Doug that K'Krah had been in a "re-education" camp for five years. We brought both K'Lai and K'Krah picture books of old slides from the 60's. They seemed enthralled and delighted. I gave K'Krah a Catholic catechism and he said, with some sense of wonder, "is this for me?" The contact was touching and so meaningful.
>
> We did not know until we got word from Gary and Doug that our friends were still alive and relatively well. It was frustrating to have to cut our visit short on the 2nd day. We felt it best for security purposes to maintain a low profile, and our driver needed to get back to Dalat.
>
> Of course Di Linh was larger with newer restaurants and businesses like the Honda dealership. But in many ways, it remained the Di Linh that I remembered, although with a more bustling market place and of course more people. The roads had certainly

improved, although we were not able to travel to one of the outlying villages as hoped. We ran out of time.

What an experience to see Di Linh again after all those years and to meet K'Lai and K'Krah's extended family. The warm and gracious reception will long be remembered in our hearts.

Jean C. Lindsay
August 17, 2016

College students, associates and professors

In January of 1998, a group of 26 individuals, college students from Manchester College, Macalester College, La Verne University and some professors traveled to Vietnam as part of the college students' course of studies. Nick Studebaker and Joel Ulrich, both cousins of Ted, were part of the group. They had never met their cousin who was a generation before them but had heard stories about Ted and were keenly anticipating this excursion.

Randy Miller described the scenario:

> We had originally begun our Asian tour in Bangkok, where we had spent five days visiting with former journalists, volunteers and others who had spent time in Vietnam during the war. Among them were Denis Gray, AP Bureau Chief in Bangkok and Lance Woodruff, another journalist. From there we flew to Hanoi where we spent 2 ½ days, then on to Hue and Da Nang with a side trip to Le Ly Hayslip's home village of Ky La. We also visited Hoi An, My Ly, Nha Trang, Dalat, Di Linh and ultimately Saigon.
>
> A day or two prior to our visit to Di Linh, we had visited a small village where the parents of one of our student travelers had lived. Madelyn Metzger was a student at Manchester College at the time. She wanted to visit the village where her parents had lived. Her father, Denny Metzger, had been a Brethren Volunteer Service worker in this village. Our tour bus stopped and all 25 of us poured out, creating quite a scene in this little village. Thanks to the creativity and persistence of our tour guide (who was with Vietnam Tourism), we found the home. Our guide asked someone in the gathering crowd if it would be okay for us to take a look around. They thought it would be okay, so we went into the courtyard and snapped a few photos of Madelyn, overcome with emotion standing in the place where her parents had lived many years ago. A few minutes later a man wearing boxer shorts and an undershirt came

out from inside the home. He was quite upset that a huge group of foreigners was milling around in his courtyard. Apparently, it had been a neighbor who had given us permission to look around, not the owner. He told us he was going to summon the police. He hopped on his scooter and sped off. I then did my best to herd our group back onto the bus and get us down the road. Thankfully, we never heard from the police.

When we arrived in Di Linh, I did not want a repeat of what we had just gone through in the village where Madelyn's folks had lived, so I suggested that only a small handful of us leave the bus to look for Ted's former apartment. Our tour guide led Joel Ulrich, Nick Studebaker, George Keeler (ULV Communications Department Chair) and me out to see what we could find. We happened onto a custodian at a small church. Our guide showed him a photograph of Ted and asked if he knew him and if he happened to know where he had lived. As it turned out, this person had been a deputy sheriff in the village at the time Ted was murdered. In fact, he said, he was the one who had found Ted. We couldn't believe our luck and followed him to a nearby restaurant/pool hall, which he said at that time had a small apartment downstairs where Ted and his wife had lived.

We went into the restaurant where this person explained our situation to the owner who granted permission for us to visit. We followed the former deputy down a narrow flight of stairs to a small doorway to our right. We entered a room that had a pool table in the center of it and beer posters on the wall. Toward the back was a small alcove, just big enough for a bed. "That was where Ted's bed had been." He explained. "Is that where you found him?" we asked. "No," he said. He led us to a small area on the floor, just in front of the alcove. "This is where I found them," he said, "His wife was lying on top of him. At first I thought she was dead too. Then I realized she was alive, and just crying. I pulled her away from him, and found that he had been shot." We stayed in that room for a while. Joel made notes. We took some photographs. Then realizing that the rest of the group must be getting restless on the bus, we made our way back, got on board and headed south.

Randy ended with the following information regarding his personal background which adds to our appreciation for this visit to Di Linh.

I grew up Brethren. My dad was a Brethren pastor and I had gone to annual conference every summer growing up. The Messenger was a staple in our house, and I had heard stories about Ted Studebaker, and how he had lost his life as a VNCS volunteer in Vietnam. I had read about him, talked with people about him (including Howard Royer, who had put together some materials about him as editor of the Messenger back then) and from what I have gathered, since the time of Ted's death, no one from the Church of the Brethren who had returned to Di Linh had been able to find the place where Ted had been killed. Apparently we were the first, and I'm glad Joel, his distant cousin, was the one to write about it for the Messenger. I remember watching Joel later that day after our visit sitting by a stream where we had stopped, writing notes in a Journal.

Randy Miller

July 2012

Joel Ulrich (Ted's cousin)

Joel Ulrich, a Macalester College student was part of the tour group that visited Vietnam in January of 1998. In the April 1998 Messenger, he described his exploration of Ted's life when he was in Di Linh.

> I want to understand war. Everyone talks about it. It seems like a phenomenon that destroys so many people's lives and leaves nothing in its place.
>
> But war is a funny concept for people in the United States under the age of 23, such as me. We have never really experienced it. All my generation has are books, movies, pictures and stories of people who have gone through war in the past. This has created a major conflict that has plagued my conscience. If I cannot understand global war, how can I possibly fathom global peace?
>
> One such story of war and peace with which many in the Church of the Brethren are familiar, is the life of Ted Studebaker. Ted, a graduate of Manchester College, declared himself a conscientious objector to the war in Vietnam. He had no hesitation, however, to entering South Vietnam in April 1969 as a participant in Vietnam Christian Service (VCS).
>
> Ted chose VCS because of its service-oriented nature, a logical extension of his Church of the Brethren background. He worked in the village of Di Linh (pronounced Z Lin) with Koho refugees who had been displaced from the mountains. He worked to increase their rice efficiency, introduced fertilizers, helped establish an agriculture cooperative and built chicken coops in bathtubs.

For an American he had a wonderful rapport with the people. After his two-year tour was completed, he decided to stay another year. He married another VCS volunteer from Hong Kong named Lee Van Pak in a church in Di Linh, the service conducted in the Koho language. They had been married only a week when Ted was killed in the lodge where he lived by a Viet Cong insurrection. The Viet Cong were national guerrilla groups fighting in South Vietnam against the government. Ted was, after all, an American, or "enemy," living among local people.

Ted has special significance to me. He was my mother's second cousin. It would be hard to get through a Thanksgiving dinner at my grandparents' home in New Carlisle, Ohio, without mentioning something about Ted and the role he represented: practicing nonviolence in the midst of violence. This cousin I never knew embodied the ideal lifestyle. I even wrote about Ted for one of my college essays on who has been the foremost hero in my life. And of course my book collection has a warn copy of the children's story by Joy Moore about the life of Ted Studebaker.

So I was elated when I heard that there was going to be a three-week class traveling to Vietnam in January, jointly sponsored by the University of La Verne and Manchester College, examining the American war in Vietnam from the Vietnamese perspective. One aspect of our 26-person trip was to visit Di Linh in hopes of finding something of Ted's life and death there.

Then I found out that my wonderful cousin, Nick Studebaker, now a student at Manchester College, was also going. The new generation of family was seeking out the old. I wanted Ted Studebaker to help me understand what war is, what it is like to die and what peace is.

I arrived in Di Linh with very little expectation of recovering anything substantial. We didn't know how to get to the lodge where he had stayed. We received word from someone who had visited Di Linh a few years back that the town was very different now from what it had been in the 1970s.

Indeed, town landscape in Vietnam had drastically changed since the late 1980s when Vietnam moved to a market economy while retaining its Communist one-party rule. Moreover, it has been only four years since the United States completely waved its trade embargo against Vietnam, a country which was then and still is today one of the poorest in the world.

So with the advent of the change to the market economy, roadside stands selling everything from rice to paint brushes to helicopters made out of Coca Cola cans are pervasive. We had been told that a market now existed in place of the old French hunting lodge where Ted had stayed.

Other things made it unlikely that we would find any trace of Ted's history. For some reason, everyone had thought someone else would bring a picture of Ted, so we ended up with no photo to show people. We also didn't know his Vietnamese name. They probably didn't call him Ted, but rather some Vietnamese derivative. It may even have been a name in the Koho language. After all, everyone he lived and worked with were Koho refugees who were no longer living in Di Linh but had now returned to the mountains.

I envisioned our group arriving in Di Linh, getting out of the bus, taking pictures of some random street and saying, "Here is Di Linh. This is where Ted Studebaker lived and died." Then back on the bus and we'd go.

We did have one lead: The hunting lodge was supposed to have stood about a hundred feet away from a church in the middle of the village, the same church where Ted and Ven Pak were married. So when we finally entered Di Linh, we stopped at a seemingly random church that we saw from our bus windows. Our guide, Hoang, got out of the bus, walked into the church, and we all waited in the bus in quiet fervor. After about 10 minutes, she came back with a small, old man who worked in the church.

"We got lucky!" Hoang exclaimed. She introduced us to Khai Tran Van (called Mr. Khai by our guide), who was a former radio operator for the Army of the Republic of Vietnam (ARVN), or the south government's military. Speaking in broken English, Mr. Khai told us that he had been asked by the ARVN to verify and document the murder of Ted Studebaker by the Viet Cong! Not only that, but he said that the old hunting lodge was indeed standing.

In a rural village it would be unusual to see close to 30 white people just walking down the street with cameras flashing and for that reason he was worried that a large group of us might attract authorities. So he said that he would only take a few of us to see the lodge. It ended up that Nick; our guide, Randy Miller and I left the bus to walk down the street with Mr. Khai.

The hunting lodge, a two story building on the slope of a hill, was now a family-owned restaurant. Out of a sense of obligation and respect, we all ordered some soft drinks and bottled water. After about 10 minutes, Mr. Khai asked the owner if we could see the rooms downstairs. The five of us went down and Mr. Khai took us into a room in the left corner by the door. He then proceeded to point to different, now imaginary parts of the room. "There was a bed here, in the corner,"

When Mr. Khai arrived that night, he saw Ted on the floor by the bed, unmoving. Ted's wife, Ven Pak, was lying beside him. At first Mr. Khai thought they were both dead, but in truth, Ven Pak was just in complete shock from what had occurred and was holding Ted as hard as she could. About 10 other officials were in the room, and there was blood all over the floor. Mr. Khai said that the "VC (Viet Cong) thought that Ted was CIA." They were afraid that he was an American Spy and were nervous about how Ted was helping the Koho people.

The room had changed a lot. There was no longer any bed in the corner, just a few chairs and a pool table, which overpowered the room. The walls were littered with posters of beautiful European-looking women holding Tiger and Carlsberg beers in their hands. Things change in 30 years. But we got lucky, indeed.

While Mr. Khai had not known Ted personally, he knew an older Koho man in Di Linh who worked for VCS with Ted. We walked down the street and met K'Krah Kaning. "You are the cousin of Ted?" he exclaimed. Family relations are quite important in Vietnam and Mr. Khai and Mr. K'Krah were very honored that two of Ted's cousins would come back to Di Linh to see where he lived.

Mr. K'Krah had been a driver and translator for people in VCS who could not speak Vietnamese or Koho languages, although he commented that Ted could speak both very well. They simply called him by his name, "Ted." He said that "Ted taught them to improve their lives, their health care and how to have a good life. People loved him very much. The Koho boys will always remember him; always remember the things he did for them."

Nick and I exchanged addresses with the two men. We took a Polaroid picture of the four of us and gave each of them a copy. I climbed back onto the bus a little dazed form the experience. I hadn't expected this.

I realize now that as this account unfolded, how a relative of mine was shot to death in the very room in which I was standing. I had felt peaceful. Something about it seemed right. Not the death, of course, but the lifestyle that Ted had lived in this village, and the comments that we heard the men tell us about his life. Ted was speaking to Nick and me through these two men. "You can live a life like this," he was telling us. "I did."

I hope to never truly understand war and peace in the same manner as my cousin Ted Studebaker did. After this journey, though, I am confident that I can contribute something in my own way to the issue of war and peace. My generation and I prove that it is possible to go through life without being in war. War is not an inevitable part of human history.

I left a little notebook paper message for Ted on the floor where he died. I told him not to worry, that a new generation of social activists was continuing his work by following the example that he, and Jesus and all other followers of nonviolence have set. Can we meet the standards that they have set for us? Or more importantly, do we dare try? As Ted ended all his letters, "Life is great. Yea!"

Joel Ulrich
Messenger, April 1998

Gayle Preheim (VNCS volunteer in Di Linh)

Gayle was Ted's agriculture predecessor in Di Linh. He returned to Di Linh with his wife Jana in 2004. Traveling with Gayle and Jana were Harley and Kate Kooker. Harley was a VNCS volunteer in the town of Dong Ha doing refugee work. He then worked in Hue at a vocational training school. Gayle described their experiences as they spent about three weeks in Vietnam, traveling overland from Hanoi to Ho Chi Minh City.

As we moved down country our route took us to Dalat and Di Linh. We drove from Dalat to Di Linh and spent a day there. We had not made contact with anyone in Di Linh prior to our visit so we were not able to meet any of our co-workers there during our visit. I did, however, want to see whether the house we had lived in back in the 60s was still there. The town itself was almost unrecognizable as we drove into it. It had grown so much.

I had been working in the Di Linh unit for about a year when Ted arrived. He replaced me, took over the initiatives that I had started and developed new programs. I saw immediately that he was asking questions about program development that I had not been asking and should have. I felt very good about him taking over when I left. We corresponded regularly after I had returned to the U.S. I of course was shocked to hear that he had been killed in the very room and bed in which I had slept. It felt surreal when I received letters from him after his death which were written shortly before.

I also had wanted to see whether we could find out anything about Ted's death and the circumstances around it. We stopped and talked with some older people who might have remembered the VNCS volunteers from years ago. We were directed to talk with a Catholic priest who was there in the 60's. After winding through back alleys, we found his residence, but he was not there. As we sat in our car in a Catholic church parking lot discussing our next move, a woman on a scooter came up to our car and inquired what we were doing there. Upon hearing our explanation, she said, "Oh sure, I remember the Americans who were here back then. I was a child living in the Catholic orphanage up the hill from the house where they lived." She led us to a house which looked very much like the picture I had of our unit house. I went to the door, knocked and a woman came. I could see past her and the layout of the house looked familiar. I explained that I had lived in the house many years ago, and asked if she knew the history of the house. She said she had not lived there for many years, but that there were "bad spirits" in the house. She would not elaborate and refused entry, although she said after lunch I should come back and she would allow me to come in. Upon return, she did not respond to my knock.

Next we stopped at a Honda dealer located a block down the street from the house. We inquired with the proprietor about any memories of the American volunteers. He said he was a boy then, and had taken some language classes with "Miss Jeanie", but knew nothing about Ted's death. However, he knew of someone who might. He gave us some tea and sent someone to find this person. When the man came, he said that Ted had been shot by a low rank-ing soldier who was a member of a VC patrol who had entered the house. He implied that this was not planned, but carried out by an undisciplined soldier. He said the man who shot Ted, he believed, was now a police officer in Hanoi. I don't know how reliable this information is, but it is one possible explanation.

Gayle explained,

The time I spent with Ted was short, but he made a lasting impres-sion on me, as he did on all who knew him, I believe. He was a cul-tural bridge builder in the truest sense of the word. He entered his new culture as a volunteer with no pretenses or presuppositions. He came with his mature sense of self, his faith and his deep sense of commitment to his beliefs. He had the skills of a masters level trained social worker, but did not foist his knowledge on to the people, or on to us who, I realize now, had not followed basic de-velopment theory as we developed our programs. With his guitar and songs, Ted was the pied piper of the unit with the community kids. He was well known and loved by many in the villages and town, even by the time I returned to the States six months after Ted came. It is hard to understand why Ted, at his young age, was called to his eternal home.

Gayle Preheim

August 9, 2016

Mackenzie Studebaker (niece)

When I was visiting in Di Linh in 2008, I didn't go more than an hour without thinking of Ted. I had an array of thoughts and wondered if there was some overlap in our paths, thoughts and impressions. Things surely must have changed since the time Ted lived there 38 years before my visit. Di Linh is no longer a village, but more of a bustling community full of commerce and transit. Yet the roads weren't paved and my attempt to make an international phone call home just wasn't in the cards.

I must have been the first red-head in a while. Walking with my new friend Truc, kids would come up to me and practice their limited English, chuckling and running back to their friends. It was real cute. They would say with a smile. "Hello, how are you?" and "Goodbye!" I wonder what it must have been like for Ted 38 years prior. I imagine he welcomed the curiosity of the local children and felt unity with their greetings. Maybe it reminded him of his little brother back home on the family farm in Ohio.

It must have been hard for Ted to put himself out there at first, to leave familiar surroundings and start a new life. Surely Ted understood that people are people no matter where you are. Although our differences may overwhelmingly surface and create a mirage of separateness, this does not diminish our bond as one human family. Ted must have understood this. He believed in the power of love and in peace. I speak of my Uncle Ted to my students when we talk about the teachings and practices of nonviolence and I feel so proud and grateful to come from a family rooted in peace and right action in the world.

I'm sure Ted loved the people and their ways. He must have thought it was so incredibly refreshing to go somewhere new in the world with a whole new set of tasks, struggles, roadblocks, experiences and relationships. Finding common ground in another culture must have been exciting. These experiences must have brought out the best of character traits in the people Ted interacted with as well as in him. I admire him for his willingness to contribute to the well-being of others, for as we are serving others we are in turn serving ourselves.

November, 2008

Gary and Doug Studebaker (Ted's brothers)

In May of 2012, Ted's brothers, Gary and Doug traveled to Di Linh. Our purpose was to simply honor Ted as representatives of our siblings (Mary Ann, Lowell, Nancy, Linda and Ron).

This journey involved three months of pre-planning as we gathered information and advice from Ted's former VNCS volunteers, IVS workers, and Ted's Di Linh co-workers. It was through these contacts that we were assisted in obtaining hosts for Ho Chi Minh City and Di Linh, finding an interpreter and reviewing ways to honor Ted that would be acceptable in this communist country.

Gary Studebaker
July 9, 2016

I was a former volunteer with International Voluntary Service in Laos. Doug and I were able to locate and make contact with some of these persons as well as others from non-government organizations (NGO). They were all interested in our travels and willing to help us with this enormous task. The networking eventually connected us with former acquaintances of Ted who had volunteered in Vietnam through Vietnam Christian Service ((VNCS), Mennonite Central Committee (MCC), American Friends Service Committee (AFSC) International Voluntary Service (IVS) Brethren Voluntary Service (BVS) and others. Contacts from these organizations led to information sharing that increased our confidence for the many responsibilities we wanted to accomplish.

The following individuals helped us with pre-planning for our visit in Vietnam:

- Lance Woodruff, formerly a VNCS volunteer is now living in Bangkok, Thailand with his family where he is a journalist.

- Richard Fuller, a former IVS worker in Vietnam has been living in Nha Trang following his volunteer service with IVS. Richard took time to personally travel to Ho Chi Minh City and Di Linh to establish hosts for us in these two cities. He also provided us with the phone numbers of K'Krah and K'Lai. These contacts were quite encouraging as we were able to introduce ourselves to Ted's co-workers and explain our purpose for visiting them in Di Linh prior to our departure. Both K'Krah and K'Lai had English speaking skills sufficient for communicating with us.

- Grace Mishler, a Church of the Brethren Global Missions worker, met us at the airport in Ho Chi Minh City. She also arranged for our housing and an interpreter to travel with us while we were in Vietnam. Our interpreter also helped by providing photography for us at the many sites where we visited.

- Mr. Hai was our host in Ho Chi Minh City. He took us to the home of the musician, Trinh Cong Son (now deceased) where we visited with his relatives. Mr. Hai then accompanied us on the 7 hour bus trip to Di Linh and stayed with us in Di Linh for two days to see that we succeeded in our objectives. Mr. Hai introduced us to his friends and our hosts in Di Linh, Mr. and Mrs. Giau.

- Mr. Giau took us to several locations where Ted had spent some time: The location of the former VNCS house, the river about a half mile behind the VNCS house, the homes of K'Krah and K'Lai and to the city of Dalat. He and his wife also invited us to their home to help us with our plans and eat with them. On another occasion he took us to a plant nursery where we purchased a tree to plant in Ted's honor.

Doug, Gary and their Di Linh host, Mr. Giau

Front: Doug, Mr. Giau's mother. Back: Bougainvillea tree planted in Ted's honor, Gary, Bo Tran, the son of our hosts and Mr. and Mrs. Giau, our hosts in Di Linh.

- Tuyen a social worker and instructor in the Social Services Department at Vietnam National University, provided interpretation on several occasions in Ho Chi Minh City. She also took us to the Mekong Delta where she gave us a boat tour of many areas along the Delta. Following this we visited with her parents who live in the Mekong Delta city of Cho Gao.

- K'Krah and K'Lai, Ted's co-workers in Di Linh welcomed us into their respective homes with a joyful celebration, food and singing. We explained that our primary concern was to keep a low profile and to minimize concern from the communist authorities regarding our visit with Ted's co-workers. Before traveling to Vietnam, we mailed to them, photos of ourselves to acquaint them with us ahead of time. However, they informed us they never received our mail. We heard similar stories of mail being intercepted and not reaching its destination in Vietnam. This incident confirmed what we had heard. We gave gifts to these two men and their families. They also gave us gifts from their culture.

May 7, 2012 Day 1

Upon arriving in Ho Chi Minh City on a hot and humid afternoon, we were greeted at the airport by Grace Mishler, the Global Missions worker for the Church of the Brethren and three National University students who took us by taxi to the hotel located on the National University campus in District One. This was an opportunity for the university students to earn credit by helping to orient us in HCMC. After getting established in our hotel room, we called Ai, an acquaintance through a friend in California. Ai brought maps for us of Vietnam and Ho Chi Minh City. She also made sure we had the appropriate electrical adapters to charge our cell phones and she gave us useful advice about places of interest in Ho Chi Minh City.

In the evening, we visited with Mr. Hai, our Ho Chi Minh City host and his family. We were warmly received by Mr. Hai and his family. After we shared, Mr. Hai, a guitarist entertained us with some Trinh Cong Son songs.

Tuyen, Mr. Hai, Doug and Gary in Ho Chi Minh City

May 8 Day 2

Grace Mishler, Tuyen and two university students took us to a day care center in HCMC, The center provided education for children with autism spectrum disabilities. The parents of the children graciously received us. With Tuyen interpreting, Gary presented the parents with some information about ways to manage children with autism from his personal experience as a special education teacher and as the parent of a child who is on the autism spectrum. At the close of this presentation Gary sang a song for them with Mr. Hai's guitar. It was a song Gary had written about his own daughter with autism. We were honored to be able to share with these parents who kindly reciprocated with words of appreciation.

In the afternoon, Grace Mishler took us to the social work department of National University where Doug spoke with the social work department chairperson regarding industrial social work, an area of his expertise. Although we had not planned for such encounters, it was a privilege to share and receive the kind reception from these individuals.

May 9 Day 3

We visited the home of Trinh Cong Son, the prolific Vietnamese singer, songwriter and guitarist whose peace songs are popular throughout the world. Before he died in 2001, he had written more than 500 songs. Many of his songs exposed the devastation of the war and the longing for peace and reconciliation. His two sisters and his niece cordially welcomed us to his home in Ho Chi Minh City. Mr. Hai, a friend of the Trinh Cong Son family arranged for and explained the purpose of our visit then gave them some background information about Ted. They cordially welcomed us and were pleased to learn that Ted had performed some of Trinh Cong Son's songs in English as well as Vietnamese. At the conclusion of our visit we were delighted to have lunch at the family owned restaurant located at the back of their home. The Trinh Restaurant is well known throughout the city.

Trinh Cong Son's niece and two sisters in front of their home

Ted began playing and singing peace and folk songs on his guitar in his adolescent years. When he arrived in Vietnam he learned some of the songs of Trinh Cong Son. One of these songs that he often played and sang in both Vietnamese and English was "Girl with Yellow Skin," a well-known song in Vietnam and beyond. Permission to print the lyrics to the song was granted by Nguyen Trung Truc and Trinh Vinh Trinh.

Girl with Yellow Skin

Girl, so young, with skin like gold,
Home you love like fields of grain,
Girl, so young, with skin like gold,
On your face fall tears like rain.

Girl, so young, with skin like gold,
Home you love, so do love the weak.
Seated there in dreams of peace,
Proud of home as of your womanhood.
You've never known our land in peace.
You've never known Olden Viet Nam.
You've never sung our village songs.
All you have is an angry heart.

Passing by the village gate,
In the night with guns booming low,
Girl so young, you clutch your heart.
On soft skin a bleeding wound grows.
Girl, so young, with skin like gold,
Home you love like fields of grain,
Girl, so young, with skin like gold,
You love home which is no more.

O! Unfeeling and heartless death.
Dark our land a thousand years.
Home, my sister, you've come alone.
And I, alone, still search for you.

Girl, so young, with skin like gold

In the evening, we walked the streets of Ho Chi Minh City and relaxed at a large park where we were pleased to see small groups of friends sitting on mats, socializing late in the evening. Upon returning to the hotel we stopped at one of the many restaurants to have a bowl of pho, a Vietnamese noodle soup of broth, linguine-shaped rice noodles, a few herbs and meat.

May 10 Day 4

Early in the morning we boarded a bus for the 7 hour bus trip from HCMC to Di Linh. We were accompanied by Mr. Hai and Tien our interpreter. The 153 mile trip was completed in a comfortable, air conditioned bus. The two-lane highway was occupied with bicycles, motorbikes and pedestrians as well as cars, trucks and buses. Therefore, it was difficult to maintain a consistent safe speed. Besides the beauty of the countryside, the passengers could watch a television show from the TV at the front of the bus. On this particular trip a Bruce Lee movie was playing. At about midway to Di Linh, the bus driver stopped at a restaurant where the passengers could relax and purchase snacks.

Mr. Giau, our Di Linh host and his wife met us when we arrived in Di Linh. They took us to the vacant lot where the VNCS house once stood. Tien, our interpreter, took pictures as we walked the grounds of the now empty lot as we realized we had finally arrived at the long anticipated location where Ted had lived.

Gary and Doug at the site of the VNCS house

Mr. Giau and his wife then drove us to their home, not far from the former location of the VNCS house. They have two daughters and one son. All three of their children no longer live at home as they are pursuing careers of their own. Mr. Giau's mother also lives with them.

Mr. Giau is a tree and rock artist. He was pleased to show us his shop and the equipment he uses to maneuver the large rocks. He cuts them into artistic designs, polishes them and sells them to art shops. Mr. Giau also creates artistic designs from the roots of large trees that he maneuvers with large machinery. These are also cut, polished and sold. Many of his wood productions are chairs and tables in his home from large tree roots.

To compliment his stone and wood designs, Mr. Giau, is also a Bonsai expert. He gave us a tour of his property of several acres to show us many potted trees which he had shaped into works of art. He took time to demonstrate how he creates these artistically shaped trees.

In the afternoon Mr. Giau drove us to the river about a half mile behind the site of the VNCS house. This was the location where Ted sometimes took the dog and cooled off in the water where children were playing.

Ted with Pudden and children at the river behind the VNCS house

Situated along the river were fields of prolific rice paddies where we rested, enjoyed the view and thought of the fulfillment Ted had experienced at this very location.

Rice fields along the river behind the VNCS house

In the late afternoon Mr. Giau and his wife took us to the home of K'Krah and his family. Upon entering the Koho village, we heard what sounded like announcements coming from a loud speaker. We learned that this was a local government official providing government information to the local people.

The gathering at K'Krah's home was very exuberant as K'Krah introduced us to his family. We showed photos to him of his work with Ted as we reminisced and talked of the past. At the same time we were amazed to realize that we were in the presence of Ted's best man, co-worker and friend. His memories and reflections of Ted remain vivid and filled with warmth. They served trays of fruit and beer to us as the sharing continued late into the evening.

K'Krah and Doug

Left to right: Tien, our interpreter, Gary, K'Krah's wife, Doug, K'Krah

Our Di Linh host had arranged for our lodging. It was a comfortable location at the home of a couple who rented rooms at the back of their property. Doug and I shared a room while our interpreter stayed in a room next to ours.

May 11 Day 5

We were invited for breakfast at the home of Mr. and Mrs. Giah where we were joined by Mr. Hai and K'Krah. We informed them that we had brought seeds from each of Ted's siblings for the purpose of having them scattered in Ted's honor. We asked for their advice on how this task could best be accomplished. We all agreed that K'Krah would scatter the seeds in Di Linh. We were pleased that they saw the significance of this task and took an interest in helping us accomplish our purpose of honoring Ted in this manner.

Dedication of seeds from Ted's siblings. Front: Doug, Mr. Giau, Gary Back: K'rah, Mr. Giau's wife, Mr. Hai

We also informed Mr. Giau and K'Krah that our family has a tradition of planting a tree in honor of a deceased loved one. We asked if such a plan would be possible in Di Linh and if so how it could be accomplished. It was decided that we would purchase a potted tree from a nursery in Di Linh and Mr. Giau gave us permission to plant the tree on his property. Upon visiting a nursery we purchased a purple blooming Bougainvillea tree, 6 feet in height. We brought it back to Mr. Giau's house where he found a spot for us to plant and dedicate the tree in Ted's honor. The fact that our Di Linh host happened to be a plant expert, gave us reason to marvel at how well this part of our trip had evolved.

In the early afternoon, Mr. Giau and his wife took us, Mr. Hai and Tien, our interpreter, to the home of Mr. K'Lai, another of Ted's co-workers in Di Linh. Mr. K'Lai, a kindly gentleman, cordially welcomed us and introduced us to his family. We brought photos of people and places in Di Linh that Ted had sent home during his VNCS years. Mr. K'Lai and his family were delighted at the wonder of this meeting just as we all were. Also in attendance was Bui, one of the flower girls at Ted and Pakdy's wedding. She joyfully greeted us and shared in the wonder of this meeting. As we sat on benches and mats on the dirt floor we again came to realize that this would be another priceless visit of friendship and sharing that Ted made possible for all of us. We all reveled in this jubilant occasion as the family served nuts that we shelled before eating and a steady supply of beer. Shortly after we arrived, Mr. K'Lai's son-in-law departed on his bicycle and came back 20 minutes later with his guitar. There were four guitarists in the crowd as we sat around talking and singing. Some of the songs were those of Trinh Cong Son. Mr. Hai, assisted us all in realizing the significance of this gathering by having us join hands as he prayed for our success in honoring our peacemaking brother. The merriment went into the late afternoon before the celebration ended. Before we departed we were sorry to learn that one of K'Lai's daughters was killed a few years earlier when her motorbike was struck by a bus on a busy highway in Vietnam.

Mr. Hai (left) prays for the success of Gary and Doug in Di Linh. Looking on with Gary and Doug are three of K'Lai's family members and Mr. Giau at the bottom right side.

**Front left side: Bui, the flower girl at the wedding of Ted and Pakdy.
Back: K'Krah. Front right side: K'Lai and his family (behind)**

May 12 Day 6

Mr. Giau's brother-in-law drove us and Mr. Giau to Dalat, a city 53 miles north of Di Linh. This was the city where Ted and Pakdy visited for their honeymoon. We traveled by fields of coffee, tea and tropical flowers which are exported to many parts of the world. Prior to entering Dalat we visited the Prenn Falls with scenic flower gardens beside the waterfalls. In the city of Dalat we toured the central shopping area and a Buddhist pagoda as well as the Bao Dai Palace. It is now a historical museum but it was the former palace of the last king and queen of Vietnam.

May 13 Day 7

We visited K'Krah at his home once again where we reviewed with him more photos of the VNCS years and asked a few more questions about Ted and his work. In the late afternoon we went sightseeing along the streets of Di Linh. We found a seldom traveled dirt road which led down a hill where we happened upon a large cemetery. Although the grounds were overgrown with foliage, it seemed to have sufficient land for continued burials. As it began to get dark, we walked back to our hotel but stopped at a restaurant along the way where we had a bowl of pho. Mr. Giau and his wife then took us to a restaurant in Di Linh to enjoy a common Vietnamese drink, black coffee mixed with condensed milk. The drink is also served cold as the coffee and condensed milk are poured over ice cubes.

May 14 Day 8

This would be our last full day in Di Linh so we wanted to make certain we completed a few more tasks. Mr. Giau took us to visit the Di Linh open market. We also stopped at the site of the VNCS house where we honored Doug's son Brett by scattering his ashes on theses grounds. Our next visit was the site of the former Tin Lanh Church where Ted and Pakdy were married. Tien, our interpreter took photos of us in front of the building which is now the Di Linh Post Office.

May 15 Day 9

Today, Doug visited a Honda Motorbike dealership which was prompted from a Honda dealership photo that Gayle Preheim had sent to him prior to our trip to Vietnam. The owner of the shop was Mr. Lai. He knew about the VNCS workers from the early 1970s. He was delighted to learn about our trip to Di Linh to honor our brother and asked us to return to his shop later as he wanted to invite another person to his shop to meet us and talk about Ted. When we returned, Mr. Lai introduced us to Mr. Thu who told us he was 14 years of age when he first met Ted. He fondly recalled that Ted was strong and could do hand stands and even walk on his hands. Mr. Thu remembered one occasion when he needed money for his family. He told us it was Ted who gave him the money. Mr. Thu informed us that he is an electrician. In their broken English, both men were very forthcoming and pleased to tell us of their recollections of Ted and their sorrow upon learning of his death. They were pleased to see photos of Ted when he did agriculture work in Di Linh in the 1970s. The sharing was a joy for us as well as these two men who were willing to take whatever time was needed to talk about Ted. They had a grasp of the significance of this landmark moment and wanted to be as responsive as possible in sharing with us.

**Standing: Mr. Lai who remembered Ted and the VNCS workers
Sitting: Mr. Thu who was a teenager when he knew Ted**

Later in the morning we visited K'Krah at the nearby Catholic Church where he serves as a catechist. At the time we visited, he was teaching a course in marriage and family with about 15 couples in attendance. When he was finished teaching we were able to share one last visit with him. At this meeting, K'Krah informed us that a Di Linh government authority questioned K'Lai after our recent visit to his home. The Di Linh authority wanted to know who the two Americans were and if we had given them any money. They also asked K'Lai the reason for our visit to his home.

We said our final goodbye to K'Krah and went across the street where we found a road that led up a hill. When we reached the top of the hill we were pleasantly surprised to discover a large school for Koho students. We were again pleased to see K'Krah's daughter, a dance teacher at this school. She took time to explain that the school is also a residence for the students while they attend school as many students live far away. The students were eager to use their English in conversation to greet us and they politely said, "Hello sir, how are you." and "Nice to meet you." The school also provides instruction to disabled students as we noted a student with cerebral palsy in a wheelchair.

As evening rain began to fall, we went to the bus station where we took a bus from Di Linh to Nha Trang, a trip of 4 hours duration and 136 miles on some steep mountainous terrain on a two-lane highway. The route took us through fertile agriculture areas where crops of flowers are grown in greenhouses. We also saw fields of coffee and tea plants growing on very tall mountains.

May 16 Day 10

Nha Trang is the city where Ted and Pakdy had visited for their pre-marital physical examination by Allen Stuckey, a medical doctor for VNCS. We enjoyed cooling off in the ocean at Nha Trang with the scenic shoreline and mountain views in the distance. This was no doubt a similar beach location where Ted and Pakdy swam and took pictures. We then visited the massive granite rocks along the coast at Hon Chong Promontory (The Rock) just north of the city. The enormous rocks as large as huge houses along the coast provided a rare scenic view of nature. Not far from our hotel were arts and crafts shops with restaurants where we ate in the evening.

May 17 Day 11

Early in the morning we boarded a train for HCMC. It was a trip of 275 miles and a travel time of 8 hours. The train was not air conditioned but it was a comfortable ride with a few stops along the way. At one of the stops vendors brought trays of food and drinks through the aisles of the train so the passengers could make purchases. From our windows we were able to see a few towns, farmland with rice fields, farmers working in the fields, oxen and water buffalo, sugarcane, vegetables and fruit trees.

We arrived in HCMC and checked back into our hotel. That evening we were invited for dinner at the home of Mr. Hai, our

HCMC host, where we visited with him and his family again. Others present were Tuyen, Grace Mishler, Tien and Lynn, a university student who was assisting Grace. After dinner, Mr. Hai gave us a tour of his 6 story home where we were treated to a scenic view of HCMC with the refreshing cool breeze of the evening from the top story of his home. As we enjoyed the pleasant breeze of the evening Mr. Hai brought out his guitar where he and Gary sang some songs.

May 18 Day 12

One of Ted's VNCS friends, Bill Herod, lives in Sen Monorom, Cambodia. We had been in communication with Bill prior to our trip with plans to visit him in Phnom Penh. In the early morning we boarded a bus and traveled to Phnom Penh. The modern air conditioned bus made the 175 mile journey in 6 hours on a busy two lane highway. At one point we forded a branch of the Mekong River on a large boat. Upon reaching the border and going through the inspection procedures, the passengers had lunch at the border restaurant before traveling on to Phnom Penh. Although the border crossing and restaurant stop took more than an hour to complete, we were simply content to have proceeded through these points with no problems.

In Phnom Penh, we discovered congested traffic similar to HCMC but we eventually arrived at our hotel. We found a shop to purchase cell phone cards which were necessary to make phone calls from Cambodia. We then visited a modern high rise shopping center where we ate at one of the restaurants. Arriving back at the hotel, we were greeted by Bill Herod where we shared with him our experiences in Vietnam and learned about his work in Cambodia. Bill works with the Bunong, an indigenous hill tribe culture in the remote mountain town of Sen Monorom in Mondulkiri Province on the eastern highland region of Cambodia.

This culture has been gradually losing their traditional ways of living as a result of war. Bill has hired arts and crafts experts and recruited volunteer workers to teach English, computer skills, math and science in this community where he enables the people to preserve their culture and receive an education.

May 19 Day 13

Our taxi driver took us to the village of Choeung Ek, one of the sites of the killing fields. From 1975 to 1979, the Khmer Rouge regime of Pol Pot arrested and eventually executed persons suspected of having connections with the former government or with foreign governments, as well as professionals and intellectuals. Ethnic Vietnamese, Thai, Chinese, Cham, Cambodian Christians, and the Buddhist monks were also targets of persecution. On the self-guided, audio tour we listened to the cruelty inflicted on these people. Death by starvation, disease and brutality was inflicted on 1.7 to 3 million innocent victims. This staggering number was one-third of the total population of Cambodia. Adding to the massacre, the Khmer Rouge destroyed 95% of the Buddhist temples. Located in the center of the many mass graves was a commemorative Buddhist shrine filled with the skulls, other bones and clothing of the victims. During our visit to the killing fields, many other tourists as well as school children were touring through this area which is established as a permanent reminder of these modern day, unspeakable atrocities.

During the Khmer reign of terror, a high school in Phnom Penh was converted into a prison called Security Prison 21. It is estimated that as many as 20,000 prisoners were killed at this location. This was one of at least 150 execution centers in the country. The site now serves as The Tuol Sleng Genocide Museum where torture and death were carried out. This is another location that has been preserved to educate the constant flow of visitors as they walk through the prison and over the grounds.

While walking through this museum we stopped to talk to two of the very few who survived the horrifying atrocities. They had each written a book about their experiences and were sitting at a table speaking with the visitors and signing copies of their book that could be purchased. The few lives that were spared in these massacres remained alive only because they had skills that were useful to the Khmer Rouge. We each bought books from these men and learned that they were artists, a skill useful to the Khmer Rouge.

We returned to our hotel that evening where our dialogue on this horrific episode continued as we shared with Bill Herod at the hotel in the evening. We also spoke with one of Bill's co-workers who as a child during the Pol Pot regime saw her father killed before her eyes by one of the Khmer Rouge. The post-traumatic stress disorder that Cambodians live with following those 4 years of massacre, continues to this day.

May 20 Day 14

At our hotel in Phnon Penh, Bill Herod introduced us to Max Ediger, a Mennonite Central Committee volunteer. The four of us walked to a restaurant in Phnom Penh. As we ate, we were interested to hear about the work Max has been doing. He has worked for peace in many locations around the world including Africa, Vietnam and Thailand as he works with communities who are struggling for peace and human rights. Max described to us some of the consequences of the war in Vietnam. We learned that Agent Orange is causing birth defects to the 4th generation and the poison is polluting the ocean just north of HCMC. This is the result of rusted barrels of Agent Orange that were buried in the ground by the America military. The toxins from these rusted containers are leaking into the ground and ocean making the water unsafe for drinking or even swimming. Through the years some American soldiers have returned to Bin Hoa north of HCMC to help clean up the poison. Some soldiers who have been carrying guilt for years have returned to ask for forgiveness and seek ways to help with the job of cleaning up.

May 21 Day 15

The return bus trip to HCMC began early. It was a comfort to arrive back at our familiar hotel. In the evening we walked the streets of the city enjoying the sights including the many vendors selling food from their carts and the variety of shops along the way. We ate at one of the many restaurants before returning to our hotel to rest up for our visit to some final landmarks in HCMC.

May 22 Day 16

Our visit continued, this time at the Ben Thanh Market, a large enclosed marketplace in the downtown area of HCMC. The many vendors here are competing to sell textiles, clothing, leather goods, handicrafts, jewelry, food from the restaurants and more.

The War Remnants Museum was opened by the Vietnamese government shortly after the war ended in 1975. The museum is located in the building of the former United States Information

Agency. Although the exhibits include anti-American propaganda, the museum provides an education to the visitor regarding a war known to the Vietnamese as the American War. Some of the many items on display at this museum are captured military aircraft, a variety of weapons, photos of the war, selected statements by U.S. politicians and military leaders, replicas of the tiger cages, statements regarding the effects of Agent Orange and other chemical toxins used in the war.

May 23 Day 17

Tuyen gave us a tour of the Mekong Delta area where she grew up. We traveled from HCMC about 80 miles south to the town of Cai Be where we took a river boat tour through some of the tributaries of the Mekong Delta. Our tour included scenic views of river boats transporting goods to the market, food service from river boats, factories that produce a variety of rice products and shops that sell arts and crafts. During one of our stops we were pleased to be entertained by Vietnamese folk singers who also presented a drama. We ended our tour by visiting the home of Tuyen's parents in the town of Cho Gao. This is the home where Tuyen grew up.

May 24 Day 18

A HCMC restaurant where we often ate breakfast was conveniently located across the street from our hotel. It was at this restaurant we gave a book ("Ted Studebaker, A Man Who Loved Peace" by Joy Hofacker Moore), to three young waitresses (probably 18 or 19 years of age) who had been helpful to us as we ordered food at this location for several days. They knew we could not read the menu and were struggling with the language each time we ordered food so they politely helped us. We explained the story about Ted by using the pictures from the book. They listened with interest as we explained Ted's work for peace, his death and our journey to Di Linh to honor him. They were delighted to receive the book.

May 25 Day 19

We visited the Reunification Palace. This was the home and work-place of the President of South Vietnam during the war. It was also the site of the end of the war when the final group of Americans were departing during the Fall of Saigon on April 30, 1975. This was the date when the North Vietnamese Army tanks smashed through the gates and occupied the palace. When tourists visit the palace today they see the spacious rooms and hallways and learn about the long history of this landmark.

Since this was our last full day in Vietnam, a going away party was planned for us by Tuyen, Grace and their friend, Sophia. They took us to one of the HCMC restaurants where we enjoyed a Vietnamese meal of pancakes served with pork, cheese and mush-rooms on lettuce. It was a delightful Vietnamese treat and a time of sharing before our departure the next day.

May 26 Day 20

In the morning we visited the spacious Ho Chi Minh City Botanical Gardens and Zoo located beside the Saigon River. This well-kept landmark contains a large variety of animals and rare plants. A stage for the performing arts is also located on the grounds where a continuous array of performers entertain the crowd at this large public attraction. On this day, the spectators were entertained with the intriguing illusions of several magicians. We were aware that this is one of the places where Ted and Pakdy visited when they first met during their VNCS language training days.

In the late afternoon we went to Tan Son Nhat International Airport where we exchanged our Vietnamese money for Ameri-can money before confirming our flights and departing for home.

Chapter 11

Memorials Honoring Ted's Work

"Preach the Gospel at all times and when necessary use words."
—ST. FRANCIS OF ASSISI

TED'S WORK FOR PEACE and justice through nonviolence has been recognized at the following venues:

CD, Ted Studebaker in Vietnam

In 2005, Steve Engle produced the CD entitled, "Ted Studebaker in Vietnam." The CD contains songs sung by Ted with his guitar accompaniment, Koho wedding music, an interview with Ted by Howard Royer and the song, "Brave Man from Ohio" by Andy and Terry Murray.

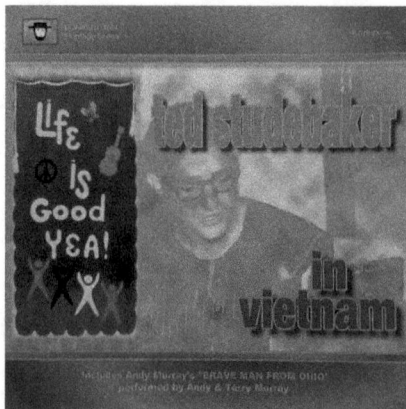

The Annual M Trophy Award at Milton-Union High School

In the mid-1970s, Ted's hometown high school (Milton-Union High School) in West Milton, Ohio, established the Ted Studebaker M Trophy Award. At the end of each school year the trophy is awarded to the senior student who has most distinguished himself or herself for determination and hard work in the field of sports and in the classroom.

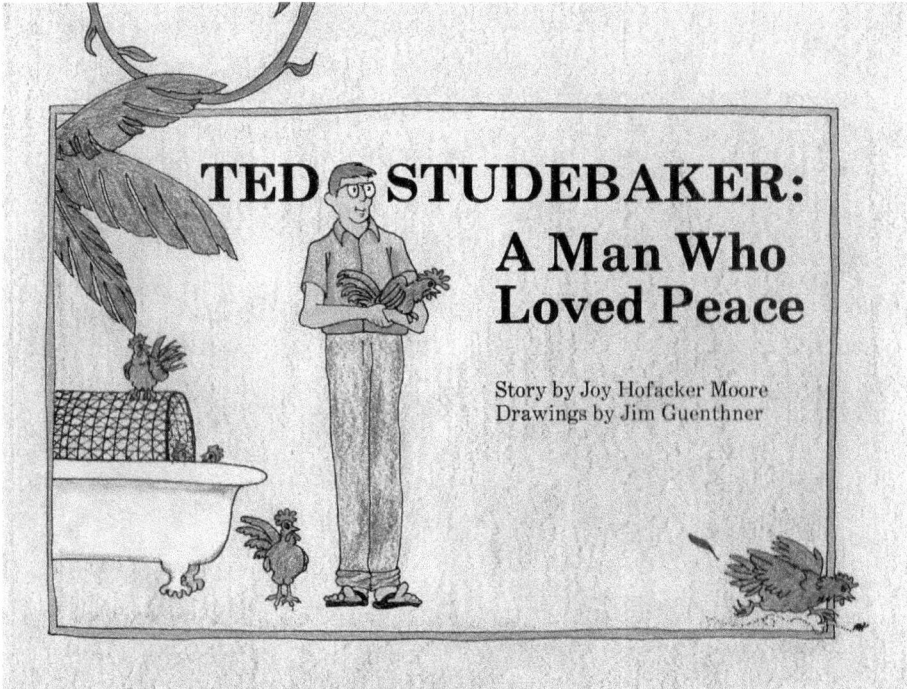

"Ted Studebaker: A Man Who Loved Peace"

"Ted Studebaker: A Man Who Loved Peace" was published in 1987 by the Herald Press. The book was authored by Joy Hofacker Moore with drawings by Jim Guenthner. The book portrays Ted's life from childhood through his work in Vietnam. It was written for readers from childhood through adulthood.

The Lion and Lamb Peace Arts Center

The Lion and Lamb Peace Arts Center on the campus of Bluffton University, Bluffton, Ohio was established in 1987 to educate the public about peace, justice, cultural understanding and nonviolent responses to conflict. Many displays of peace are presented through works of art throughout the campus. The Granite Memorial Wall is one of the displays at the Honda Outdoor Peace Sculpture Garden. The names of many peace heroes are carved into the wall including that of Ted Studebaker. Guided tours provide school age children as well as adults with an opportunity to learn about peace by interacting with art, literature and music.

**Peace Heroes Wall at the Lion and Lamb Peace Garden
at Bluffton University, Bluffton, OH**

The Dayton International Peace Museum

The Dayton International Peace Museum in Dayton Ohio was founded in 2004 for the purpose of inspiring a culture of peace. Among the many displays of nonviolent peacemakers is the permanent display honoring the work of Ted Studebaker with audio visuals, artifacts, and narratives that depict his life and work for peace and justice. The museum educates the public through peace walks, speakers, music, literature, art and multimedia productions. They are equipped to broadcast programs as well as educate visitors through virtual and interactive exhibits.

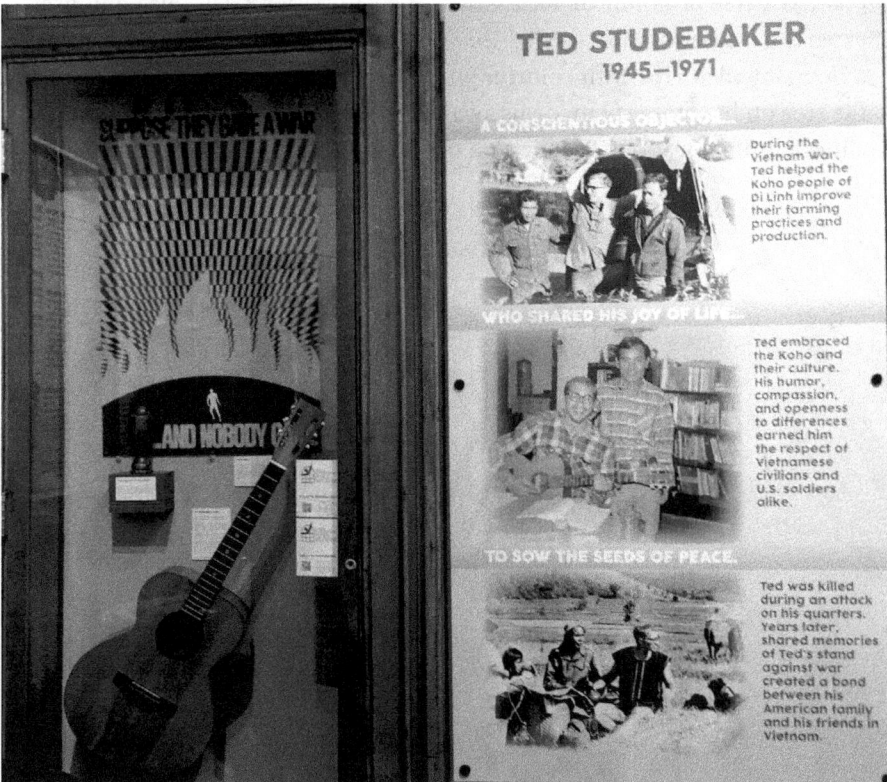

Dayton International Peace Museum

Drama

In 2008, Don Parker wrote and directed the drama, Life is Great, Yea. The drama portrays the events in the final week of Ted's life in Vietnam and his work for peace and justice. The drama has been presented at church venues and has been produced on a DVD.

Tree dedication in Di Linh, Vietnam

While Ted's brothers were in Di Linh in May of 2012 they purchased and planted a tree in honor of Ted's work. Their host, Mr. Giau (also a bonsai expert) gave permission for the tree to be planted on his property. It was a Bougainvillea Tree with colorful purple blossoms. His invitation to plant the tree on his property made us aware that we could not have planned for a more fitting location to dedicate a tree in honor of Ted.

Tree in honor of Ted's life in Di Linh, Vietnam

144

Seeds of Peace

Gary and Doug asked each of their siblings to supply them with a packet of seeds to take with them to Vietnam where they would be scattered in Di Linh in Ted's honor. It was agreed that Mr. K'Krah, Ted's co-worker and best man would perform this task, symbolizing the seeds of peace that Ted sowed. They are also described in the scriptures:

- Productivity—Matthew 13:8
- God's Word—Luke 8:11
- Eternal Life—John 12:24-25
- Abundance—2 Corinthians 9:6
- Peace, Righteouness—James 3:18

Gladys Muir Peace Garden

In 2014, Ted's work was recognized with a plaque on the Peace Wall of the Gladys Muir Peace Garden at Manchester University, North Manchester, Indiana. Ted was honored as one of the alumni from Manchester University for his contributions to peace and justice.

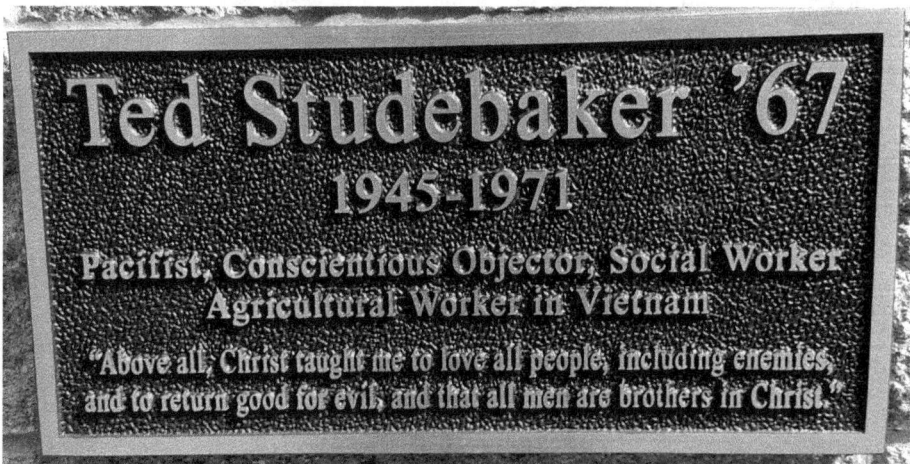

Gladys Muir Peace Wall, North Manchester, Indiana

145

Bethany Theological Seminary

In 2015, Ted's work was honored at Bethany Theological Seminary in Richmond, Indiana. A brick in the memorial courtyard is inscribed with words of admiration from Ted's Siblings.

**Courtyard at Bethany Theological Seminary, Richmond, Indiana.
Photo courtesy of Bethany Theological Seminary**

CD, Heroes and Friends

Included on the CD, Heroes and Friends is the song, "An Instrument of Peace" honoring Ted's life and sung by Jackie Bisin. The CD was produced in 2015 by Tim Kerns. The songs were written by Gary Studebaker.

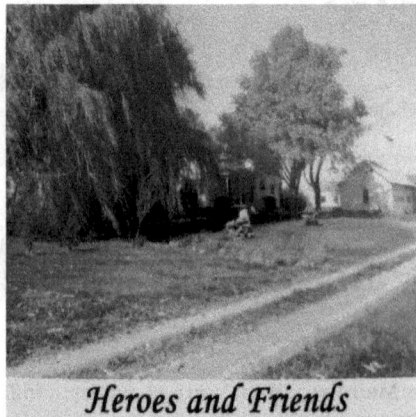

"An Instrument of Peace" on the CD Heroes and Friends, 2015

Hall of Honor Award

In 2016, the Milton-Union Alumni Association honored Ted's work for peacemaking with a plaque bearing his photo and descriptions of his work. The plaque is displayed on the high school Hall of Honor Wall. It reminds students, staff and visitors of Ted's work for nonviolent peace.

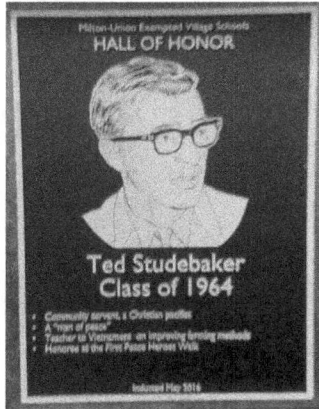

Hall of Honor, Milton-Union High School, West Milton, OH

Ted's siblings at the high school Hall of Honor ceremony.
Front: Nancy Smith, Mary Ann Cornell, Linda Post
Back: Gary, Ron, Doug and Lowell Studebaker

"An Enduring Force for Peace"

Ted Studebaker: An Enduring Force for Peace is the biography of Ted's life, written by Gary and Doug Studebaker.

MEMORIALS HONORING TED'S WORK

Date	Ted Studebaker Timeline
September 29, 1945	Birth. Ted grew up on the family farm in southern Ohio, involved in school, church, sports and farm responsibilities in his childhood years.
May 24, 1964	Graduation from high school, participated in athletics, prepared for a life of social service, declared his position as a conscientious objector and stated his intent to serve in a nonviolent capacity.
June 12, 1967	Graduation from Manchester College in 3 years with majors in psychology and sociology. During these years Ted worked and studied in the college heat plant, participated in sports and the deputation team.
March 21, 1969	Graduation from Florida State University where he earned a Master's Degree in Social Work.
April 7, 1969	Entered Brethren Volunteer Service training at New Windsor, MD
May 12, 1969	Arrived in Saigon, Vietnam to begin work through Vietnam Christian Service, took eight weeks of language training where he met Pakdy, also in class.
July 21, 1969	First day in Di Linh, Vietnam for orientation by agriculturalist, Gayle Preheim, begins learning to speak Koho, makes plans for agriculture work.
April 17, 1971	Wedding day. Ted and Pakdy both signed on to serve a third year in Di Linh through VNCS.
April 26, 1971	Death. Forces opposing the Americans entered the VNCS house, shot and killed Ted. Shortly thereafter, memorial services were held in Saigon, the West Milton Church of the Brethren and on the family farm where Ted's ashes were scattered.
Ongoing	See chapters entitled Pilgrimage to Di Linh and Memorials Honoring Ted's Work.

Chapter 12

Remembering Ted

"There may be times when we are powerless to prevent injustice, but there must never be a time when we fail to protest."

—ELIE WIESEL

Co-workers, Relatives and Friend's Remember Ted

Bill Herod (VNCS colleague)

Bill, the assistant director of VNCS, came to Manchester College during Ted's senior year to recruit volunteers. Bill wrote the following poem shortly after Ted's death.

Ted

We first met at Manchester College
In Petersime Chapel.
Home between tours,
I was there to speak about Vietnam.
Ted was on his way over.
He had come to listen-
And learn what he was getting into.
Someone had told me
That he would be there,
But I didn't know which one he was
Until time for questions.
Ted asked many questions.
They were all very serious,
Searching
Practical questions
Of a fellow who wanted to know,
Essentially,
Whether it was really possible
To work constructively
In such chaos.

Also, Ted wanted to know about
Identification.
Was it really possible to be accepted
As an individual,
A friend,
A brother;
Or were you always
Just
Another
American?

I saw Ted many times in Vietnam
But I remember him best
At Di-Linh.

Once when I visited,
We waded in mud up to our ankles
Carrying bread up the hill
To a little school.
Ted stopped here and there
To chat with friends
Along the way.

It was good to be with Ted-
To listen to him
Switch easily
From English
To Vietnamese
To Koho,
To watch him,
Just as easily,
Laugh with the neighbors,
And tease the girls,
And play with the kids.

It was good to be there with Ted,
Because you know
That he belonged.
Ted and I talked about his questions
From months before at Manchester.
He had found his answers.
No absolute answers,
To be sure,
But answers you could
Live with.

Then,
Suddenly,
Like the splendor
Of a tropical sunrise
It was Ted and Pakdy

The two were one
After two years of
Hop-scotched courtship
Meeting in Tuy Hoa,
Or Nha Trang
Or Di Linh
Or Saigon
And filling the spaces
With letters
And dreams.

Their joy in living
Was not the kind you envy,
But the kind you share,

And then
The day so suddenly begun
Was suddenly ended.

It was the classic intersection
Of eternal opposites
As the warrior's bullets
Smashed into his chest
And he reeled back
Into the closet
Where he had once raised
Baby chicks
Death is neither new
Nor ever far away.
Sometimes it seems as though
All we get out of life
Is Death.

There is,
Of course,
The knowledge that
Ted was very much a man

And nothing more-
Doomed from the day of his birth
To die somewhere,
Sometime.

And there is,
Of course,
The resurrection miracle working
Even now,
To secure for Ted
His place
Among the very much alive
(Who of us who know him
Can ever be the same?)

He would not want us
To do him the ultimate injustice
And remember him
As a sinless saint.
No, Ted was human,
Like all of us,
And we dare not think lightly
Of his struggle.
And yet there is,
Deep in each of us,
An emptiness
Which grows
When those we love
Are no longer
Where we need them.

An emptiness
Which expands
In proportion
To the pointlessness
Of the losing.
When good men fall-

Casualties of their own virtue-
Rage has no place.
But what, then?
We are left wandering-
Like Ted's hand
Fingering the frets
Of his guitar
Searching for just the right chord
To begin
An unfamiliar peace
Soon the strings vibrate
A little,
And there is harmony
As we begin to deal with Ted
In his mystical transposition.

The song takes form
As we realize
That we must
Pick it up,
Join in,
Carry on.
Only that gentle harmony
To which Ted
Attuned his life
Can help to fill
The silent void which,
With his going,
Now remains.
Death is neither new
Nor very far away.
And now we begin to know
That what we get out of death
Is life.

Donald Sensenig (Missionary with Eastern Mennonite Board of Missions and Charities)

I am still moved by Ted's dedication to improve the lives of people in a difficult situation, despite the risk to his own life. Besides having that kind of dedication, he was also a fun guy. We played occasional games of tennis when he was in Saigon, among other interactions. He seemed to enjoy hanging out with our small group of missionaries.

Martha Henderson (VNCS colleague)

When I heard about Ted's death, I was devastated and disillusioned! I went to my favorite place to pray and cry, The Rock, Hon Chong, in front of Chan Y Vien Tin Lan. As I prayed and cried, God sent me the scripture in Matthew, "Go ye into all the world baptizing in my name, and lo, I am with you, even until the end of the world." Matthew 28:19–20. I recognized that Jesus' message was the Great Commission and he did not promise anything but his presence, not freedom from death, but his presence. This was a poignant revelation and reassurance to me.

Marcy Ninomiya (VNCS colleague)

Ted, Gloria Redlin and I were in language study together when we first arrived in Saigon. I have fond memories of Ted playing his guitar late at night. I would join them and we would sing for about an hour most evenings from about 10 to 11 pm. Gloria, a VNCS nurse was killed in October of 1970. How ironic that both of them lost their lives in Vietnam. I have reflected on that fact numerous times and how I am the only one of the three of us who left Vietnam alive. Our favorite song that we sang every time we sang was "Lord of the Dance." To this day I think of Ted and Gloria whenever that song is sung.

Betty Vos (VNCS colleague)

I did not know Ted well as he worked in Di Linh and I was based in Saigon. But, my husband and I went to Di Linh twice, once in September of 1969 when we were nearly finished with language training and all of us were sent "up country" for a couple of days to rely on our new skills and again, a week before he was killed, to attend his wedding. A van full of us drove up from Saigon. I knew Ted was a true and delightful embodiment of what it means to be the presence of Jesus in the world.

Howard Royer (Messenger editor and interviewer of Ted in Di Linh, Vietnam)

Four months before Ted's death, Howard Royer from the Church of the Brethren General Office, traveled to Di Linh where he interviewed and observed Ted at his various work sites. Howard saw Ted's interaction with the Koho and his colleagues during his time in Di Linh and other parts of Vietnam. Howard's insightful account is the only interview with a report of Ted's day to day experiences in Di Linh and other parts of Vietnam. His description (below) appeared in the June 15, 1971 Messenger.

Ted Studebaker: A Dissenter from Despair

"Cool it and don't fret; this boy knows what he's doing."

These were among the parting salvos of Ted Studebaker as he left his Ohio homeland in the spring of 1969 for Brethren Volunteer Service and Vietnam. In effect, the sentiment was voiced by Ted again this spring from Vietnam, in a letter he wrote late on April 25 to critics back home. It was the last letter Ted was ever to write.

Raided:

That night shortly after mid-night the residents of the Vietnam Christian Service unit at Di Linh, South Vietnam was shelled with B-40 rockets, blasted with a plastic charge, and raided by Viet-cong soldiers. Three women who had made it to the bunker of the stairs of the old hunting lodge were not harmed; Ted, still in his bedroom, later was found shot to death. For him two years of creative interchange in the lives of the central highland people in and around Di Linh, and a commitment to a third year of service had come to a tragic end.

Among the three women who had survived the terror was Ted's wife of one week, Ven Pak, a volunteer from Asian Service who Ted had learned to know in language training in Saigon. Their wedding, which had occurred a block down the road from the Vietnam Christian house at the Koho Tin Lanh Church eight days before, was a festive occasion not only for the church but for many in the wider community.

Enriched:

It was in that community, 140 miles northeast of Saigon, that I had spent a couple of days with Ted some four months before, observing what he was trying to do in a foreign land. One of my clearest impressions was that Ted scarcely seemed a foreigner there; because of his own simple tastes, because of his proficiency in both the Vietnamese and Koho languages and, perhaps above all, because he felt genuinely enriched by the culture of those around him, and sought to learn from that culture, Ted was very much at home.

This at-homeness became increasingly apparent as I saw how he related to neighbors, local officials, teachers, pastors, priests and peasants in our trek from village to village and door to door. It was discernible through his enthusiasm for his work: the demonstration paddies where he had greatly increased the yield of native rice, the taste of which the villagers strongly preferred over new improved varieties; the improved brooder house where he was readying 200 Pilch baby chicks for distribution to villagers; the cooperative store he was helping local people establish; and his trust in and encouragement of the Montagnard members of his VCS team.

Obstacle:

In love as he was with the people and the land, Ted was far from accepting what was happening to their lives. "The biggest obstacle to development work in Vietnam is simply the war itself," he told me as a thousand yards from us American piloted helicopter gunships loaded ARVN troops likely destined for a search mission back in the hills. It was from back in the hills that thousands of Montagnard tribesmen have been driven, forced to trade their once lush farmlands for "temporary" villages and less productive paddies along the main road. Here, among these refugees, Ted's efforts in agricultural development were directed.

While historically the Montagnards have been the outcasts of Vietnam, the anguish Ted felt was that now they have become pawns in the program of pacification and Vietnamization. Their home areas in the highlands had become the free firing range for both Vietcong raiders and American and South Vietnamese bombers. What is at stake ultimately, Ted felt is their survival as a minority.

In striving to learn of the traditions and values of the Montagnards, Ted came to respect them greatly. He knew at a glance, the personal and cultural characteristics that distinguished the Montagnards from their Vietnamese neighbors. He valued the primitive tribesmen not only for what they might become, but for what they were. It was no surprise to learn the best man at his wedding was a Montagnard—K'Krah, a teammate in VCS and close personal friend and that the service itself was in the Montagnard's Koho language.

Mistakes:

In two days of travel together Ted and I went from Saigon to Nha Trang to Bao Loc to Di Linh to Dalat. Seemingly the most insecure area was the section in and around Di Linh. Ted was relaxed, though, as long as one did not need to be on the road at night or did not get detained while traveling close to American military convoys. He told of shellings now and then into Di Linh and other villages, and of mine explosions, making children and other innocent persons the victims of war. "Sometimes," he commented, "it seems like this whole war is run on a bunch of mistakes."

On occasion, as we traveled Ted talked of his upcoming plans for marriage. He and Ven Pak had announced their engagement in Vietnam, but had yet to break the news to Ven Pak's parents, which meant a journey to her home in Hong Kong and to Ted's family in the States. Actually Ted earlier had written his parents about it, but in Koho, the dialect no one at home could read.

When I last saw Ted in Dalat, he told me that he hoped that in this highlands town, which is a beautiful blend of Vietnamese and French influences, he and Ven Pak would honeymoon in the spring. His hope was fulfilled; that is how he spent part of this final week of life.

Because Ven Pak was on a project quite some distance from Di Linh, I did not meet her. I did feel I had come to know her, however, through the snap shots Ted shared and through his own resplendence when he spoke of her.

Common Qualities:

Upon meeting Ven Pak at the Studebaker home near Union, Ohio early last month, the day before Ted's memorial service, what surprised me most was how many of Ted's qualities seemed to be her own. The gentleness, the humility, the sincerity, the warmth, the determination were readily conveyed. Even more so, her life statement shared with the directors and staff of Vietnam Christian Service seemed to echo what Ted himself might have written:

"I'm sure all of you share my grief over his death, but I hope you will grieve even more for those who do not understand what he did."

The real story of Ted is not only of his life and death in Vietnam; it is also of his years of growing up in Ohio's "Studebaker Country;" of his feel for the soil and things of the farm; of his devotion to high school and college football and other sports; of swimming in the farm pond; of parents who expect their children to do their own thing, to leave the family nest and to make their own mark in the world; of older brothers, one of whom was in military service in Germany, another in Brethren Voluntary service in Morocco and a third, in International Voluntary Services in Laos; of three sisters and a younger brother all of whom make their contribution to the families sense of solidarity; of studies and friendships at Manchester College, where he earned his way through school and did four years work in three; and of masters study in social work at Florida State University.

"Good Hunting":

Ted's story is closely aligned with the West Milton Church of the Brethren, where in a sermon in August 1967 he stated his feelings about the war. Holding up a newspaper clipping of a starving, homeless child, he read an accompanying article which said, "Hunting was good today in the Mekong Delta region. U.S. Marines bagged 45 of the enemy, wounded scores and completely wiped out one small village."

"Hunting is good today!" Ted responded. "Just like the sportsman who comes back from a day of hunting rabbit and pheasant shooting. So many rabbits, so many pheasants, he lays them all out to see. The dehumanizing process of war concerns me deeply. What can I do about Man's inhumanity to man?"

While in Vietnam Ted continued to be in contact with his home church. "Second only to my family," he wrote a year ago, "you as representatives of the West Milton Church of the Brethren are responsible for my thought and actions concerning conscientious objection to the military, my pacifistic views and my volunteer service. Without the church, as skeptical as I am about it now, I might find myself in a uniform as part of a giant military machine whose reason for existence seems based on economics and a big myth. The meaninglessness, the wastefulness, and the non-necessity of this war are outweighed only by its inhumane effects, both here and in the States. "I do not pretend to understand all the whys and wherefores of this crisis, but one thing stands out clearly in my mind. This war is immoral and wrong, and the burden of blame is upon the U.S. military, the U.S. government and the U.S. people. I believe there is a lot of truth in the statement that the killing will stop only when American public opinion demands it."

Response:

This letter was printed in the Troy, Ohio Daily News. It prompted a Troy couple to write Ted of their disappointment in his stand, questioning his understanding of the Bible and wondering even if the organization, Vietnam Christian Service was "Christian." The couple appealed to Ted to study the word of God, to spurn the company of those misfits who call the war "immoral," and "for God's sake, to get your views straight."

Only hours before his death, Ted replied, thanking the family for writing, indicating the difficulty of debate by letter, and clarifying only one point. "I do not 'feel the enemy is right' any more than I feel the U.S. military is 'right' here," he wrote. "I believe strongly in trying to follow the example of Jesus Christ as best I know how. Above all, Christ taught me to love all people, including enemies, and to return good for evil and that all men are brothers in Christ. I condemn all war and conscientiously refuse to take part in it in any active or violent way. I believe love is a stronger and more enduring power than hatred for my fellowmen, regardless of who they are or what they believe.

Sincere:

You probably think I'm pretty idealistic and by your letter indicate that I'm a pretty mixed up kid. But, I cannot apologize for any part of the letter I wrote to my church, since it well represents honestly and sincerely my feelings and concerns about this particular situation. I have tried to speak from both experience and reason, not from mere emotion or hearsay."

The letter was closed by Ted thanking the family for writing and for expressing concern for his welfare. "Please know that I am in excellent health and adequate safety. I know I am a fortunate man and life is great to me."

Affirming life:

Excerpts from the letter, the statement of Ven Pak Studebaker and tapes of guitar playing and singing which Ted had recorded only weeks before in Vietnam were used by Pastor Phillip Bradley in the memorial service on May 3. On the altar of the church were two Bibles—Ted's heavily marked edition in English and Ven Pak's in Chinese, a Brethren Service cup, a shovel, Ted's guitar and a banner lifting up in essence the affirmation with which he had concluded the final letter and many letters before it: "Life is great, yea." It was on this note that Ted Studebaker, 25, a dissenter from despair, a champion of love, a man of peace, came home. He had lived his life purposefully. To the nation, the community, the church, the loved ones, his return was not unlike his leaving; it simply put meaning to the words:

"Cool it and don't fret. This boy knows what he's doing."

Howard E. Royer

Keith Weidner (Ted's High School English Teacher)

Keith Weidner's description of Ted was printed in the Troy Daily News on April 24, 1971.

> I was numbed by the news of Ted Studebaker's death in Vietnam. All day my thoughts had been dominated by a nameless, unidentifiable depression, as if my own life had in some subtle way been dominated by the sacrifice of his.
>
> I see, as if in the confusion of a dream, a series of muddled impressions—a cheerful, smiling, vibrant alive boy in my classroom among others very much like him; a red-jerseyed competitor, a fierce and jarring tackler on the gridiron; a willing and unstinting giver of himself in class projects; a good humored and uninhibited performer as one of the "Other Brothers" in his Senior Assembly—impressions conjured up as an admiring and appreciative teacher and class advisor.
>
> Then I see the committed humanitarian, as depicted in a newspaper photograph, "doing his thing" in Vietnam out of love and compassion for a hapless, helpless and hopeless people. And now I am reminded that such images as these are all that we have left of Ted Studebaker.
>
> How did this happen? Why this unarmed, unselfish, unsullied and unsung servant of his country, his God and his fellow man?
>
> As usual, the questions come more easily than the answers; and when one ponders the imponderable perhaps the most he can hope to accomplish is a kind of acceptance if not a solution. Ted followed his conscience into a conflagration whose smoke has clouded the judgement of many good and wise men and whose heart has warped the perspective of a righteous and God-fearing people.
>
> Who are the heroes of this kind of confusion? Perhaps they are those whose love of country arms them with zeal and weaponry to oppose an enemy in combat regardless of personal costs. Perhaps.
>
> Are they the Calley's of this world who, caught up in its madness, blindly doing what their myopic vision hazily reveals their duty in spite of higher laws to the contrary? I pray God they are not.
>
> Or are they the real heroes whose convictions enable them to strip off the varnish and veneer to see the very core of things, the basic and eternal truth of the brotherhood of man and then lay it all on the line in support of this conviction? Yes, these are the heroes; but who sings for them?
>
> Such a man was Ted Studebaker, though I am quite certain that he did not view himself as a hero. His route to Vietnam was,

after all, a personal one, charted carefully by his conscience and illuminated by his belief. Once there, he gave all he had to give. Small wonder I feel so diminished.

Lowell Studebaker (brother)

I always regret not knowing more about Ted's early years as he was 13 years my junior. No doubt his growing up on the farm was very similar to each of us eight siblings and involved hard work and responsibility tempered with church, Sunday school and of course sports. My more intimate knowledge of Ted and his life burst onto my radar suddenly the day he was killed in Vietnam. He had compressed his education, training and preparation into a few short years in order to serve a poor, hurting and disadvantaged group of Montagnard people in the highlands of Vietnam. The fact that war raged throughout the country would not be a deterrent to Ted. He would not consider himself important, brave, significant or special, yet he was all the above and more as he became one with the Montagnard people of Di Linh, Vietnam. Knowledge of a life well lived has created forever memories of Ted in my heart.

Nancy Smith (sister)

Ted was the 7th sibling in our family and first to be born in a hospital. At birth the Dr. had to facilitate his breathing.

My children, Alison and Philip had a very fulfilling relationship with Uncle Ted. As young children they recall his fun and loving nature while teaching them tricks and playing with them in the yard at the farm.

I believe Ted's peace journey began with his family background and Christian upbringing in the Brethren teachings of pacifism. Mom and Dad fully supported his beliefs and his giving nature. He even engaged in ways to settle differences in his own family as a young child. Ted's confidence and courage in the presence of war, led him to a hill tribe in Di Linh, Vietnam, where he established many friendships and was highly respected. He had the courage to live his beliefs which came through in his writings, "He who takes a stand is occasionally and often wrong, but he who never takes a stand is always wrong". Ted showed us by example that actions speak louder than words. His life has made us stop and think about how we can become better people. Jerry Leggett said, "A Peace Hero is often an everyday person who accepts risk and succeeds in making the world a less violent and more just place." That is why I admire this peace hero.

Linda Post (sister)

At the age of 23, my brother, Ted courageously lived his beliefs by standing firm in his desire to help those in need through nonviolence in the midst of war. As a young child he was influenced by the Bible and God's teachings. In a presentation to his home church, he spoke of the need to love all people, including enemies and to return good for evil. He knew love was more powerful than hatred.

His skills in agriculture and social work were a perfect fit for serving the needs of the people in Di Linh, Vietnam. Through these efforts and his language proficiency he developed deep and lasting friendships. Ted was in his element and as he said, he was a privileged man to have the opportunity to serve as he did.

Few of us have the courage to stand firm in our beliefs, especially when that stand is unpopular and dangerous. His courage to live his beliefs is an unforgettable example of love and courage at addressing the needs of mankind. Ted would never consider himself a peace hero, but that is truly what he is.

Gary Studebaker (brother)

I used Ted's own statements and actions to compose the song, "An Instrument of Peace" (lyrics below). Since Ted was not willing to stand by in silence in the face of injustice and he would not allow war to interfere with his nonviolent actions for peace, he accomplished what the war could not as expressed in his own statement: "Christ taught me to love all people, including enemies, and to return good for evil and that all men are brothers in Christ. I condemn all war and conscientiously refuse to take part in it in any active or violent way."

An Instrument of Peace

An Instrument of Peace
That's what I choose to be
Wherever there's injustice Lord
Keep me ill at ease
Let me serve nonviolently
Where there's a human need
For I must stand on God's command
And sow the seeds of peace

Refrain

For I will build trust where there's
suspicion
Hope were there's despair
Laughter in the village
Music in the air
Love where there is hatred
Comfort where there's pain
With simple acts of kindness
Let peace and justice reign

Let it rain, let it rain
On the seeds of peace we sow
Let them flourish in the highlands
And the valleys down below
Let them grow in our hearts and minds
So everyone will know
Peace becomes reality
When the seeds of peace we sow

I'll gladly work for peace
Not built with tools of war
I'll not stand by in silence
With injustice at the door
When faced with inhumanity
You will sometimes stand alone
Yet peace will never be secured
Till seeds of peace are sown

Refrain

Yes I will build trust where there's
suspicion
Hope were there's despair
Laughter in the village
Music in the air
Love where there is hatred
Comfort where there's pain
With simple acts of kindness
Let peace and justice reign

Let it rain, let it rain
On the seeds of peace we sow
Let them flourish in the highlands
And the valleys down below
From those bold, peacemaking heroes
There's a simple truth we know
Peace becomes reality
When the seeds of peace we sow
Peace becomes reality
When the seeds of peace we sow

Doug Studebaker (brother)

On October 11, 2014, a ceremony was held at the Gladys Muir Peace Garden at Manchester University where a plaque with Ted's name and one of his quotes, was added to the Gladys Muir Peace Wall. Doug made the following presentation at this ceremony.

> I'd like to begin by expressing our family's gratitude to Manchester University, the Gladys Muir Peace Garden and to Katy Brown and her staff at the Manchester Peace Studies Program for inviting us (Ted's family) to be a part of this honor given to our brother. We have so looked forward to this day. Also today we are honored to be here with Robert McFadden as he too is celebrated for his contributions to peace and nonviolence Robert we say congratulations.
>
> I'm Doug Studebaker, Ted's little brother. I've been asked to say a few words today on behalf of our family. I'll begin by introducing my siblings:
>
> - Mary Ann Cornell—Troy, OH
> - Nancy Smith—Troy, OH
> - Ron Studebaker—Ashville, OH
> - Gary Studebaker—Anaheim, CA
>
> And unable to be here today with us:
>
> - Lowell Studebaker—Loudon, TN
> - Linda Post—Bremerton, WA
>
> We are a close-knit family of 8 siblings who grew up on our parents' farm north of Dayton near West Milton, Ohio. Without a doubt our parents, Stanley and Zelma, are smiling down on this gathering today with so much pride and gratitude. Now if Ted were with us today I'm sure he'd characteristically be quite modest and brief. Possibly he'd say, "Gee, I want to thank you all for coming and for this honor. But it really wasn't anything so special that I did. I was just trying to help these folks in the Central Highlands of Vietnam who were so adversely affected by this war. And for me it was just a great experience to be there with them. Guess it was just my time to go . . . "
>
> Now I do want to take a moment to acknowledge the irony that I am speaking here at Manchester on behalf of our family. You see it's a remarkable fact that every member of our family including our parents attended Manchester University. That is every

member except for the last guy. That would be me! So I'll simply say this to my siblings: "I somehow seemed to find meaning in my life in spite of this glaring short coming!"

Family remains priority for us and we gather every year without fail for our annual Studebaker Sibling Bed & Breakfast event somewhere in the country. This year in Vancouver, British Columbia marked our 19th year. It is so special for each of us to do this.

We remember vividly 43 years ago as we learned of Ted's death. We immediately gathered at the farm and how we clung to one another for 5 days grieving, crying, singing, laughing, remembering and then celebrating our brother's life. We knew then as we'd known before that there was something very special about this life, what Ted had accomplished in his 25 years and what he grew to firmly stand for. We would soon learn what his life had meant and now continues to mean for so many others, many of whom we'll never have the opportunity to meet.

So we as siblings remember Ted as:

- The quiet, easy-going brother who worked hard on the farm and in all he pursued.

- As "my big brother" who grew to be the biggest/strongest among us.

- The one who was so fun loving and likeable.

- The athletic one who was "poetry in motion" on ice skates playing hockey on the farm pond in winter, a ferocious competitor on the football field and a gifted pole vaulter in the days following the Reverend Bob Richards and before fiberglass. Ted was the guy that you wanted on your team, not just because of his talent, but because of the supportive team player that he was.

- A gifted musician (guitarist/vocalist) who was drawn to the folk and peace songs of the 60s and later to the anti-war songs of the Vietnamese activist singer/song writer Trinh Cong Son. As with my own son who shared Ted's middle name, I recall how Ted's music seemed to transport him to a very special other worldly, meditative place. A place where he would enviably reside for minutes on end.

As has been so well chronicled today, Ted's life seemed to gain momentum, focus and a sense of urgency as he departed for Manchester, Florida State and then the war-torn Central Highlands of Vietnam. He went to this war with a guitar and a shovel, and not a gun.

Brad Yoder (Manchester University professor)

Brad Yoder from the Department of Social Work at Manchester University presented the following remarks at the Gladys Muir Peace Garden ceremony on October 11, 2014:

> We are here today to recognize and to honor the life and work of Manchester University alumnus Ted Studebaker. I want to welcome again the members of Ted's family and other guests who are with us today.
>
> I feel deeply honored to try to summarize Ted's life in a few minutes today. Though I never had the privilege of meeting Ted personally, we had many of the same interests and concerns as farm grown, peace-making, conscientious objecting social workers in the 1960s. I have been moved and inspired by those I have talked with who knew him and worked with him here at Manchester University, during my travels in Vietnam, in conversation with family members and friends.
>
> It is clear that to understand what shaped Ted into the person he became we need to begin with his family. We are grateful for those of you who are able to be with us today to honor Ted in this way. From many sources there is broad and consistent evidence that the Studebaker family was very close and that within the diversity of the family there was a deep love, a profound respect for and support of each person as an individual in their own right. What a gift of nurture and growth that has been.
>
> Ted was strongly shaped by the West Milton Church of the Brethren and in turn had a profound effect on the congregation. He shared much about his struggles and his vision during the 1960's regarding the United States involvement in Southeast Asia and what he should do about that. That dialogue began well before Ted decided to go to Vietnam through Brethren Volunteer Service to work with Vietnam Christian Service and it continued while he was serving right up to the end of his work.
>
> At Manchester Ted developed his own Fast Forward program to graduate in three years, long before Manchester had a Fast Forward program! He chose courses which reflected his interests and the future direction of his life such as Urban and Rural Community, Race and Minority Relations, Social Welfare, Cultural Anthropology and Human Geography. Ted had a vision which extended well beyond his comfortable territory of Ohio and Indiana and was preparing to act on his vision.

166

Ted continued his development by getting his Master's Degree in social work at Florida State University then prepared to go to Vietnam. In his newly adopted country Ted quickly came to adapt to living and working in a different culture in the midst of the conflict and chaos of a society being shattered by war. Ted's special interest and commitment were to the Montagnard people of the Central Highlands, who during the best of times were a marginalized minority in Vietnam. Ted not only learned the country's primary Vietnamese language, but also became fluent in the Koho language of the people he worked with around the town of Di Linh. He came to love the Koho people and made their struggle his own.

Patiently developing a network of close relationships, Ted applied all the knowledge and skills he had gotten from growing up on the farm in Ohio to his study at Manchester and Florida State as an agricultural development leader. He especially worked with local partners to increase food production through new strains of rice, nurturing bees and raising chickens. Anyone who has had the opportunity to visit the Di Linh community including Church of the Brethren Messenger editor, Howard Royer, Ted's brothers Gary and Doug and I have been moved by Ted's ongoing influence more than 40 years later with friends like K'Krah, K'Lai and Mr. Thu. They say, "We trusted him," and "We loved him so much as he loved us and our own land." They remember the green bike Ted rode around to visit the various projects.

During Ted's two plus years working in the Di Linh area, he met Ven Pak (Pakdy), a fellow Vietnam Christian Service volunteer from China. Over time she became the love of his life and they were married in Di Linh. Tragically as we all know, Ted was killed one week after they were married. It's sad that their time together was so short, but aren't we grateful that they had that time together.

Among the themes that recur throughout Ted's life including his service in Vietnam are:

1. Working expediently to pursue his goals

2. His attraction to simple living

3. Creative use of whatever resources were available to him, and

4. His commitment to peacemaking and nonviolent social development of every person, every group, every people.

Ted understood many kinds of human knowledge about agriculture, plant genetics, human geography, group dynamics, cultural stability and change, international politics, crisis theory, conflict transformation and military conflict. He integrated all to improve the quality of life for the Koho people of the Central Highlands of Vietnam.

Ted could reduce very complex situations down to a clear and right course of action. He was a big-picture person, who brought life down to the importance of each interaction with each person in each moment.

At Manchester now we often say that we want our graduates to be persons of ability and conviction. Ted was all of that at such an advanced level that we can't capture Ted's words. Ted was the personification, the incarnation, of the goals of a liberal arts education at Manchester University. We can only respect and admire him, point to him as a model and say thank you for the privilege of being part of trying to preserve and pass on his legacy.

Julia Lutz (niece)

Ted was 8 years older than me and when I would get to spend the night at Grandma Zelma's house I remember my uncles always doing athletic things like running races or walking on their hands across the room. This was amazing to me since I don't have an ounce of athleticism in my bones. I remember Uncle Ted skating on the pond with other boys and playing hockey. I also remember Uncle Ted helping with chores around the farm like milking cows. He tried to teach me how to milk a cow once but I was too afraid I was going to hurt the cow. I also remember Uncle Ted and Uncle Gary bringing some milk in the house right after milking the cows and getting me to take a sip . . . yuck.

The last time I saw Ted was at our house on Market Street in Troy. Mom invited Uncle Ted and Uncle Gary to bring their guitars before Ted left for Vietnam. Mom played the piano and Ted and Gary played their guitars while Milton and the six of us kids gathered 'round and sang. Mom still has a picture of that gathering.

Uncle Ted was a man who truly lived his beliefs and was not afraid to do so. I have always admired him for that. God had a plan for Uncle Ted and his plan lives on.

Jill Morris (niece)

Ted's life had a profound effect on me. It was my first experience with death and the wonderful example the Studebaker family showed me. I recall the day we spread Ted's ashes as we gathered at the farm under the willow tree, beside the spring as we threw the ashes to the wind. I recall a wind swirled the ashes up in the air. It was as though God was indeed with us. On the banner at the church memorial service was the statement, "Forgive them." Ted reminded us to love our enemies. As the family talked about Ted, I remember tears but I also remember laughter. Grandma was sure that the butterfly at the window was a sign from Ted to her from God that Ted was safe in heaven. What a testament of faith and the goodness of God!

Not long after that event, I lost a friend in a motorcycle accident and the loss of my first born child. The loss of Ted helped me cope with loss and has given me a better understanding that we will all go in our time and that God is with us. I have looked up to Ted as a hero since my early years.

Amy Powell (niece)

Ted's love of music and his spirit and ability to love everyone made Ted a hero to me. He played guitar songs with piano accompaniment at family gatherings. Uncle Ted showed us that for him, killing was not an option. He fought to educate, to show love and to reveal Jesus through his actions toward others who were considered enemies by many. To me, Uncle Ted was like Jesus in the flesh. I admired him with my limited knowledge of war at age 10 when he was in volunteer service, but I never realized that he was in any danger.

I was very excited and happy for Ted and Pakdy when they got married. Then about a week later I got the news that he was killed when enemy forces opposing the Americans, entered the house where he was living. I remember how angry I was and how I cried not understanding how this could happen. Didn't they understand he was there to help? I went through some questioning with God. Where was He during this time?

Now I know that God was there all along. Uncle Ted listened to God's voice and followed. As much as I wish I could sit down and have a conversation with him, I will forever be grateful for the legacy of love and grace that he showed me through his life's work and passion. The reality is that Uncle Ted's story continues to speak to my heart many times and he has influenced my life for the better.

Alison Henson Bucchi (niece)

We moved to Ohio when I was in the third grade and our family spent a lot of Sundays at Grandma and Grandpa Studebaker's home. I remember Ted's nice smile. He was fun to be around. He was very athletic and would walk around the front yard on his hands. It was even more impressive when he would walk up and down the front porch steps on his hands.

Ted with Alison and Philip, his niece and nephew

Shortly before we moved back to Ohio he joined Brethren Volunteer Service and left the country. While he was in Vietnam, I wrote a letter to him and he wrote back:

April 29. 1970
Di Linh, Vietnam

Dear Alison,

I was happy to receive your letter and was interested in your comments about my work and my beard. You know Alison; I really don't like rice wine at all. As a matter of fact I've gotten stoned (ask your dad about this word) on it a few times, but drinking rice wine is part of the custom of the Koho people and so to be polite, I have been obligated to partake now and then. Following your implied hint, I will definitely practice moderation more faithfully after this. As for my beard, no reason, just that every young man likes to be different and show others a new face once in a while. You might be interested that the Vietnamese people have very little hair on their arms and bodies and cannot grow beards unless they are very old. I suppose this is because it's very hot here compared to America, so they don't need hair to keep warm. I plan to shave soon.

I am glad you're following current information with the new IR-8 rice. I've experimented with it here but have found little success in Di Linh because we are in the mountains and the cooler weather does not favor this variety. In other places in Vietnam, I've seen it grow quite well.

I just returned from a two week vacation in Vietnam. I traveled to many places and would like to tell you about it sometime. I tried to travel by road in Vietnamese vehicles as much as possible, a real interesting experience.

Alison, I must say goodbye for now and go to work. Thank you for writing. How is the family and how do you like school?

Love,

Ted

Ngac yo (Goodbye in Koho)

He sent to me a beautiful little beaded bracelet which I often wore. I still have that letter and bracelet saved in a little wooden box.

Alison's bracelet, a gift from Ted

I was going to Concord Elementary School when he was killed. I was given a message that Phil and I were to go to Aunt Mary Ann's house after school. This wasn't an uncommon after school occurrence as I was taking piano lessons from her at the time and I went there weekly. But when I arrived this time it was different. Mary Ann and Mom gathered us in the family room and tearfully told us the news. It was tough to hear and see how hard it was on the adults. I'm sure at the time I could not grasp the gravity of the situation. I just recall the cousins were all kind of stunned.

I also remember a butterfly story. After Uncle Ted's death, Grandma was upstairs cleaning one of the bedrooms. She noticed a butterfly outside the window. The butterfly kept fluttering near the window and eventually landed near the sill. When Grandma looked closely at it she noticed it was like no other butterfly she had ever seen. It had black and white stripes and a streak of red.

Now that I am teaching at Milton-Union Elementary. I have met a few people who knew Uncle Ted. Joy (Hofacker) Moore teaches first grade and knew Ted through the Church of the Brethren. She wrote a book called, "Ted Studebaker: A Man Who Loved Peace." Linda (Coate) Miller went to Milton-Union High School with Uncle Ted. She told me he was the nicest boy and very good looking!

Clearly Ted was a well-respected young man who was well liked by every person who came in contact with him.

Philip Smith (nephew)

I was probably only 6 the last time I saw Ted. I do remember how skilled he was at walking on his hands. I was so impressed that I had to learn myself. I can picture him entertaining the people where he lived in Vietnam with his skill. He was always making sure everyone was having fun and he was interested in what I was up to. I have vivid memories of him playing tag with us at our house. I can picture Ted's face in our hallway like it was yesterday. I will forever remember when I heard about his death. It was my earliest memory of loss.

At my young age of 8, I didn't understand war and peace missions but I recall my sunken heart at the thought that I would never see or play with Uncle Ted again. His legacy encourages me to want to serve others in my life. It was a comfort for me to meet Pakdy. It was a wonderful experience for her to be with the family after Ted's death.

One time cousin Dave and I were skinny dipping in the pond when we saw Grandma Zelma and Pakdy walking down to the pond. There was no time to get out so we just stayed in the water and had a "pleasant conversation" as they pulled up a lawn chair. We must have been in the water for a half hour!

Mackenzie Studebaker (Ted's niece)

In 2008, Mackenzie Studebaker, Ted's niece, traveled by ship to many cities around the world including Ho Chi Minh City, where her ship would be docked for 5 days as part of her international studies through Syracuse University. Upon reaching Vietnam it was Mackenzie's desire to travel to Di Linh to be in the town where her uncle Ted had lived 39 years earlier. In Ho Chi Minh City she went to the bus station and purchased a ticket for the seven hour trip. While she was at the station she met Truc, a Vietnamese girl about her age. Truc spoke English and asked if Mackenzie was going to Dalat, the town of her destination 53 miles northeast of Di Linh. The girls became acquainted and traveled together to Dalat. They became friends and stayed in Dalat the first night.

The next morning Truc was kind enough to go with Mackenzie back to Di Linh to help her find someone who knew Ted. They made many inquiries about Ted but were unable to find anyone who was knowledgeable of Ted after 39 years. Still, Mackenzie was inspired to be in Di Linh, the town where Ted had lived. She stated, "I simply wanted honor him and to explore this area where Ted had established friendships and made agriculture contributions as a volunteer." She and her friend Truc exchanged contact information and continue to maintain an ongoing friendship through written correspondence.

Verda Mae Peters (aunt)

Ted brings to mind his athletic abilities of ice hockey and basketball as well as board games he played with my children. Also Ted taught my son, Bruce how to play the guitar. It was Ted who reminded us, "I have never heard of a president pinning a medal on a pacifist." Because there is so much super patriotism, I recently wrote this to the editor of our Hillsboro newspaper. "Besides the constant praise for active soldiers and veterans, I would like to see some praise for the humanitarian aid workers who also make sacrifices to bind up the horrible wounds of war."

Paul Peters (cousin)

Growing up in Union Ohio, I always cherished Sunday afternoons after church. The Peters and Studebakers always got together. In the summer months, my brother Bruce and I always marveled at Ted's ability to pole vault in his yard. He and I were closest in age. Bruce and I watched him, but could never do it.

We all spent many hours on the pond playing ice hockey together. Sometimes we had exciting Monopoly games. I will never forget those treasured memories. Ted was not only my cousin, he was my best friend.

Bruce Peters (cousin)

These are some of the enjoyable times Ted and I shared on the farm during our early years. He was an exceptional guy.

1. He was a talented pole vaulter. I tried it but could never do it like Ted.
2. We built forts in the barn using straw from the hay mow.
3. We swung on the rope from the tree then leaped in the pond.
4. In the winter we ice skated on the pond.
5. We got in the empty silo, threw a golf ball against the silo wall then tried to escape being hit by the ball.
6. Ted gave guitar lessons to me.

Phyllis Cribby (VNCS colleague with Ted in Di Linh)

On June 20 2013, Ted's siblings and their spouses had a reunion with Phyllis Cribby at her home in Gresham, Oregon as they wanted to spend time with Ted's friend and trusted VNCS colleague. It had been 42 years since Phyllis had come to the Studebaker homestead with Pakdy. Ted's siblings held the fondest of memories of her through the years. As they embraced Phyllis and listened to her share stories about Ted's work and their mutual support for one another, she was a reminder once again, of her comforting presence as she shared with the Studebaker family at the time of Ted's death many years ago.

We realized how privileged we were to meet with Phyllis in June of 2013. In April of 2014, less than 10 months after our visit with Phyllis, she passed away at the age of 82. The significance of this reunion would be a lasting memory for each of Ted's brothers and sisters. Immediately after the sentimental reunion with Phyllis, she wrote a letter of appreciation expressing her fondness for this momentous occasion in her life. We informed her that the feelings were mutually shared.

Phyllis Cribby at the reunion with Ted's siblings in Gresham, Oregon, June 20, 2013

From the reunion with Phyllis, Ted's siblings also learned more about her life of service that included volunteer work beyond her years in Di Linh. At the time of Ted's death, she spent one week with the Studebaker family followed by several days with her family in Grants Pass, Oregon. She then returned to Di Linh to continue her health care work. This time she lived in an apartment a few blocks from the previous VNCS house. She continued her work there for about one year then was assigned to provide nursing care in a hospital in Kontum, Vietnam, a town 320 miles north of Di Linh. She worked in Kontum for about two years when she and all of her VNCS colleagues were forced to evacuate Vietnam due to the 1975 take-over of Vietnam by the military forces from North Vietnam.

Before Phyllis provided nursing services in Di Linh, Vietnam, she had served for 2½ years as a Peace Corp volunteer in Andhra Pradesh, India. During this part of her life she worked in a nutrition program with a team of other health care volunteers. Following her many years of work as a nurse, she returned back to her home in Oregon where she continued to make contributions in the area of health by advocating for a cleaner environment in the state of Oregon where she was pro-active at investigating environmental issues and educating the public through her writing and speaking engagements.

Chapter 13

NGO Volunteers Who Died
in Vietnam and Laos

"Blessed are the peacemakers, for they will be called children of God."
—JESUS OF NAZARETH

THERE WERE MANY OTHER non-government organization volunteers besides Ted whose life ended in Southeast Asia during the war in Vietnam. These volunteer workers were either killed in war, killed in a plane crash, vanished or drowned in Vietnam or Laos between 1962 and 1973. These were volunteers from the following non-government organizations: LWR, MCC, AFS, VNCS and IVS. These men and women were all in their 20s. All were highly educated and well qualified in their field of expertise and all provided life sustaining services in impoverished and war-torn countries. Most of the following individuals were reported by Stuart Rawlings in his book entitled, "The IVS Experience From Algeria to Vietnam." Permission was obtained from Stuart Rawlings to record this information herein.

Daniel Gerber

On May 31, 1962, Daniel was abducted as he was walking on the grounds of a Vietnamese hospital with his fiancée, Ruth Wilting of Cleveland, Ohio. Wilting watched as Gerber's hands were bound and he was led away. Gerber, 22 years old at the time of his abduction, grew up on the family farm in Kidron, Ohio. In lieu of military service he had chosen to serve a three-year term with the Mennonite Central Committee as a leprosarium worker in a Vietnamese hospital in Ban Me Thuot, Vietnam. Gerber's attitude about war and peace was stated simply in his application to MCC: "Christ taught love and that is what his children must do." Through the years since then there were both promising and disappointing reports regarding Gerber's whereabouts. Nothing could ever be confirmed. Twenty five years after Daniel was missing, a friend of Daniel's, who went on to be a missionary in Japan, came to see Daniel's mother. He told how he prayed for Daniel every day. One day the Lord told him, 'Daniel is with me.' This statement in 1987, helped bring closure to Daniel's mother.

Peter M. Hunting

Peter was killed in an ambush in 1965 while serving through IVS in Vietnam. He stated, "I wanted to serve my country through IVS, not the military." Peter was a graduate of Government Studies at Wesleyan University. He served as IVS Regional Leader in Vietnam. His favorite books were *India: The Most Dangerous Decade, Syntactic Structure*, and *Winnie* the Pooh. In 2009, Jill Hunting, Pete's sister wrote a compelling book entitled *Finding Pete*. In this book Jill rediscovers the brother she lost in Vietnam.

Max M. Sinkler

Max died in 1966 while serving in Vietnam when his jeep was hit by an army truck. Max was an agriculture graduate of the University of Illinois and Oklahoma State in Plant Pathology. His favorite reading was *U.S. Foreign Policy and How to Win Friends and Influence People*. He wrote, "I would like to see these countries develop democratic societies because there is a danger in authoritarianism."

Michael Murphy

Michael served in Laos and drowned while crossing the Mekong River in 1966. He was an Electrical Engineering graduate of Catholic University and a member of the National Honor Society. He served with IVS in Laos. His favorite reading was *Growing up Absurd, The Psychology of Loving, Commonweal and Commentary*. He wrote, " . . . there is a job to be done, and I am personally bound to act."

Dennis L. Mummert

Dennis and two Lao veterinarians were killed in an ambush while driving from Vientiane to Paksane, Laos on August 5, 1966. Dennis was an agriculture graduate of the University of Illinois. He was an IVS volunteer in Laos. His favorite books were *Black Like Me* and *The Other America*. He wrote, "To me, the search for world peace is not through a gun barrel . . . "

Arthur D. Stillman

Arthur was in the same vehicle with Dennis (above) and was also killed when ambushed while driving from Vientiane to Paksane, Laos on August 5, 1966. Arthur received his B.A. from Harvard and his M.A. from Yale in Southeast Asian Studies. He spent two years in Thailand with the Peace Corps, and he served as a Peace Corps Training Officer. He was the IVS Associate Chief of Party in Laos. His favorite reading was *Elements of Social Organization, National Geographic* and the *Journal of Asian Studies*. He wrote, "I want to serve my country without having to harm other human beings."

Richard M. Sisk

In 1967, Richard was killed in Phan Rang, Vietnam. He was a graduate of Paul Smith Junior College and the Louisiana Polytechnical Institute. He served through IVS in Vietnam. His favorite reading was *Tree Growth* and *Forest Science Magazine*. He wrote, "I owe a debt to our way of life, and I want to pay for it by working through IVS."

Martin J. Clish

In 1967, Martin died when his plane was shot down over Laos. He served through IVS in Cambodia and Laos. He was a member of the International Farm Youth Exchange in India and an agriculture graduate of Bethany Lutheran Junior College and the University of Wisconsin. He served in Laos as the Associate Chief-of-Party. Martin listed his book preferences as *Young Americans* and *A Nation of Sheep*. He wrote, "Understanding is the basis on which we can build world peace and security."

Frederick D. Cheydleur

Fred and his Lao assistant were assassinated on March 25, 1967. Frederick D. Cheydleur, 21, of Orchard Lake, Michigan was slain by Pathet Lao dissidents. He was a Quaker pacifist who served as a village development worker and was involved in the distribution of improved rice and seeds when he was killed. Fred was involved with Fellowship House and Tolstoy Farm before coming to Laos. His favorite reading as stated on his application was *Coming of Age in Samoa, The Mind as Nature, The Hot Air Machine* and *Popular Mechanics*. On his application, he wrote, "I want to face the problems that face the world, and I want personal harmony with that spark of good that is in each of us."

David Gitelson

In 1968, David was taken prisoner and shot. He was an agriculture volunteer in Vietnam. David studied soils at the University of California and was a medical specialist in the army. His favorite reading was *Six Plays* (by Odets), *Six Plays of the South*, (by Green), and *I. F. Stone's Weekly*. During his IVS service in Vietnam, he was known as my ngeo (the poor American).

Chandler Scott Edwards

On April 24, 1969, Chandler and his two Lao assistants were killed in an ambush while serving in Laos as a volunteer worker through IVS. He was a graduate of East Tennessee State University. His favorite books were *The Ugly American, The Prophet* and *Freedom's Death*. Chandler stated, "I prefer to relate to people and be with them for their possible aid but not in a dictatorial leadership role."

Gloria Anne Redlin

Gloria, a VNCS nurse, was killed in Vietnam just six months before Ted Studebaker was killed. Gloria from Oshkosh, Wisconsin, worked as a nurse for Lutheran World Relief in VNCS. Gloria and Sergeant Louis Emil Janca were traveling by Moped to Dr. Pat Smith's hospital in Kontum City late at night on October 13, 1970. On the way, they went through an ARVN roadblock without stopping. It is believed they were unaware that the patrol forces were friendly. There is also speculation that Sergeant Janca was the intended victim of an assassination. Sergeant Janca was killed and Gloria was mortally wounded. Gloria died of her wounds eight days later on October 21, 1970.

Ted and Gloria were in language training together in Saigon for eight weeks. Many evenings Gloria and Marcy Ninomiya, both VNCS nurses enjoyed singing songs as Ted played the guitar. One of the songs they especially liked to sing together was "Lord of the Dance."

Alexander D. Shimkin

On July 14, 1972, Alexander was killed by a grenade in Quang Tri, Vietnam. He graduated from Indiana University in History and Government. He had previously worked in hospitals and on rice projects with IVS in Laos. His favorite readings were Faulkner, Dreiser, political science and American history. He reported on the unfair treatment of the people in his area who were being used to clear minefields. He wrote "I have no right to be exempt from making sacrifices overseas."

Richard Thompson

Richard had been working for the American Friends Service Committee's medical rehabilitation center in Quang Ngai, Vietnam. Richard was an expert with tools, machines, electricity and repairs. He learned Vietnamese so he could negotiate and run errands for the team. Richard stated, "instead of observing a drama at its climax where justice triumphs and villains are overcome, I am a participant in the absurd. I have stepped behind the looking glass." In November 1973, Richard escorted two girls who were paraplegics to a home in Saigon, where they would live and receive medical care. During his return flight traveling from Saigon to Quang Ngai, a city 350 miles northeast of Saigon; Richard was one of the 23 passengers who were killed when the airplane crashed into the side of a mountain during stormy weather. Richard felt morally obligated to help the victims of this war.

Chapter 14

Summary

"The best way to find yourself is to lose yourself in the service of others."
—MAHATMA GANDHI

AS WE HAVE LEARNED from the previous chapters, Ted and many volunteers like himself were willing to work to advance economic and life-sustaining goals through volunteer work. Seldom are these individuals viewed by the mainstream of society as individuals to be recognized or honored, nor do they seek acknowledgement or acclaim for their work. It was President Kennedy who recognized the commitment of the conscientious objector when he stated, "War will exist until that distant day when the conscientious objector enjoys the same reputation and prestige as the warrior does today."

Ted knew he must be true to his conscience and God's call in his life. Although his belief and that of a soldier were in opposition to one another, he accepted the soldier and knew that he too was obeying his beliefs. He shared with some of the soldiers in Di Linh, at opportune times (as previously described) because he knew that honest dialog was necessary for understanding. Exclusion of such persons because of their beliefs was contrary to Ted's views and he made that known publicly. Yet he was openly critical of those in positions of authority who presented no logical defense or rationale for supporting a war that results in ongoing calamity and futility with no end in sight. This is still the case in Vietnam although that war was fought decades ago. The unintended consequences of the war in

Vietnam (known as the American war in Vietnam), is an ongoing reality. (see Chapters 8 and 14).

When we visited The War Remnants Museum in Ho Chi Minh City we noticed a display that depicted photos of children with birth defects linked to toxins used during the war. We saw photos of many children, three generations after the war, with deformed limbs, missing limbs, tumors, enlarged heads, vision problems, inability to grasp, no head control and no bladder control. The United States and private groups are providing some physical and financial help to clean up the toxic pollutants left behind by the American military. American soldiers that were adversely affected by toxins from the war are receiving government help with some of their medical expenses. When looking at the photos of the medical devastation alone, mankind is left to make a moral judgement about the war in Vietnam as Ted expressed so many times before he arrived in Vietnam and during the war.

Ted concurred with a quote from Viktor Frankl, "Life ultimately means taking the responsibility to find the right answers to its problems, and to fulfill the tasks which life constantly sets before us." Ted was not conformed to the world, nor did he see the need to go along with precepts that contradicted his Christian beliefs and background from which he was nurtured. It was obvious to him that taking a position simply to be "politically correct" was indefensible. He understood that taking a position that goes "against the grain" of accepted thinking would involve persecution as were many others who went before him. He had read the lives of Jesus Christ, the Apostle Paul, Dietrich Bonhoeffer, Thomas Kempis, Mohandas Gandhi, Martin Luther King and others.

For Ted and many others, being a pacifist is unrelated to being passive. These selfless individuals see an injustice and are willing to do something about it, not with force, yet they remain a force. Ted never sought recognition yet he remains a hero for taking a bold stand for peace. Billy Graham recognized the influence of such courage and stated, "When a brave man takes a stand, the spines of others are often stiffened."

The history of nonviolent peace workers and the opposition they faced including being killed is well documented. Yet their contributions to mankind are renowned and the list of these heroes is long. Many of these courageous men and women are honored in biographies, peace gardens, on peace walls, halls of honor and memorial landmarks. Ted's conscientious objector beliefs and work for peace and justice were openly challenged by some individuals. There was opposition to his letters of rebuttal to publication editors. A letter from a person back home rejected him and his organization (VNCS) as not being Christian. Countless others chose to simply remain silent rather than to challenge him or enter the arena of injustice and human rights. Some individuals find a "comfort zone" in not "making waves" or not taking a stand regarding these issues.

Yet we saw that Ted welcomed the encounter and was gifted with a confident defense of his positions as well as self-control at tactfully communicating his rationale regarding war and peace. In doing so he was able to live out his beliefs with a sense of purpose and fulfillment at addressing life's central issues which eventually he died for. Khalil Gibran addressed this position when he stated, "You would know the secret of death. But how shall you find it unless you seek it in the heart of life." Thus, Ted had reason to confidently state, "When we can really live out our religion, when we can honestly love our neighbors as ourselves, then I think things will really begin to pop . . . our reason for being here would take on new meaning and purpose." Indeed his characteristics as well as his first hand experiences of working in a war zone put him in a position to express himself on these issues without compromise. It is intriguing to speculate how he would have carried on these same human concerns wherever his future vocation would have taken him. It may have been the continuation of exposing injustice and addressing problematic social issues regardless of the vocation he would have chosen.

Ted was perceptive when sharing with people by making his message palatable. He realized that we are often influenced by personal biases that render our judgments neither genuine nor truthful. After one of Ted's speaking engagements, he was asked by one of his listeners if he had personally met Christ. He responded by telling the person to ask someone who knew him well: his boss, a relative or a neighbor. He knew that others could more objectively answer that important question. His answer also conveyed the wisdom of being impartial.

Ted's brother, Ron reflected on Ted with these comments:

> Simply stated, Ted chose the high road led by his conscience, to freely give of his love and talents to his neighbors in a war torn land. He was fully prepared and armed with confidence in the mission that God had set before him. He was totally committed to give of himself without reservation. His own life of faith spoke volumes through his actions for which he gave his all.

Ted gratefully acknowledged his government's position at accepting alternative service as a way to serve mankind as opposed to military service. He wrote to his draft board, "I don't feel unpatriotic or disloyal to my country. However, I do think there are certain rights, beliefs, and values to which one should be more devoted to than his country if he has arrived at them through conscientious thought, learning and experience."

Ted made statements about the war in Vietnam that were supported by many accounts. Below are some of the accounts:

Ted's statement: " . . . it concerns me today that some people—important people in high offices and positions, are so mistaken about how to live with their fellow man; sincerely mistaken."

> Account: In his 1995 memoir, In Retrospect: The Tragedy and Lessons of Vietnam, Robert McNamara, stated, "We were wrong, terribly wrong. We owe it to future generations to explain why." Robert McNamara was the Secretary of Defense during the war in Vietnam from 1961 to 1968 under Presidents John F. Kennedy and Lyndon B. Johnson.

> Account: In the New York Times article of June 29, 2001 entitled, "Lying About Vietnam," Daniel Ellsberg stated, "Johnson couldn't face being accused of losing a war. Instead, he stayed in and lied about the prospects. That made for a prolonged war, an escalating war and essentially a hopeless war."

Ted's statement: "The meaninglessness, the wastefulness and non-necessity of this war is outweighed only by its inhumane effects, both here and in the States. Sometimes, it seems like this whole war is run on a bunch of mistakes."

> Account: In 2004, the Rand Corporation reported that up to 30% of all UXO (unexploded ordinance) failed to detonate in Vietnam. Total clean-up costs are projected to be as high as $140 billion dollars. The total cleanup of UXO may never be achieved.

> Account: On May 6, 2012, Wyatt Olson reported in Stars and Stripes, " . . . since 1975 about 40,000 people have died from un-exploded ordinances (UXO) and 66,000 have been injured and maimed according to the Vietnam Ministry of Labor, Invalids and Social Affairs.

> Account: On February 17, 2016 Nicole Weisensee Egan reported in People Magazine that Kim Phuc continues to receive laser treatments to alleviate the pain from skin burns she received 44 years ago during the war in Vietnam. In 1972 at 9 years of age, she and her family took refuge in a South Vietnamese Temple when she was struck with napalm bombs.

Ted's statement: "I can't by any stretch of reason, see how the U.S. can ever hope for an honorable end to a dishonorable, illegal and immoral war that it is fully responsible for starting. The sight of the U.S. government in Vietnam continually scalds me. How could the US be so damn stupid?"

> Account: In the August 5, 2014 Business Insider, Harrison Jacobs reported that the 20 million gallons of highly toxic chemicals that the U.S. Military sprayed on Vietnam, still saturates Vietnamese lands, wildlife and groundwater. These toxins continue to inflict birth defects for generations of Vietnamese children after the war.

> Account: On July 22, 2015 Brian Handwerk at Smithsonian.com reported 40 years after the last Marine left Saigon, some 271,000 veterans of the war may still have full post-traumatic stress disorder (PTSD) and for many vets, the PTSD symptoms are only getting worse with time.

Ted's statement: "I wish for more moratoriums in the US, on the war. That may be the only way to end the war. The politicians talk about an honorable end to it."

> Account: On March 29, 2013, Michael Ip, from ABC News reported that growing anti-war sentiments and sustained casualties, pressured President Nixon to bring an end to the war in Vietnam. On November 13, 1972 he began to give in to the pressure to end the war. He then started to plan an exit with National Security Adviser Henry Kissinger and Maj. Gen. Alexander Haig.

On two separate and unrelated occasions during our visit in Di Linh, we heard Mr. Giau and later, Mr. Lai make similar, yet enlightening comments to us as they remembered the American War. They recalled the destruction that was done to Di Linh lives and property. After our meeting with Mr. Lai at his Honda dealership in Di Linh, he sent an e-mail to Doug.

After I met you and your brother yesterday, I have many ideas in my heart. During the war I used to think American families were not closely linked with each other. When I saw your family, I realized I was mistaken. You traveled a very long distance to come to Di Linh to honor your brother, Mr. Ted, who died here. The local people loved him very much. He was a good man and we hold his friendship close to our hearts. We remember Mr. Ted with love.

Your friend,

Lai

Mr. Lai saw the death and destruction by American military forces in his own village of Di Linh. The war imparted feelings of mistrust, dissention and the impression that American families do not care for one another. Decades later when Ted's brothers traveled to Di Linh to honor their fallen brother, Mr. Lai was emotionally moved and shared his feelings of love and appreciation at such an act of love. He admitted his honest misconception about the bond that connects American family members.

It was during the war in Vietnam that the American military commander, General Westmoreland, made a glaring misrepresentation when he stated, "The oriental doesn't put the same high price on life as does the Westerner."

The consequences of war as exposed in these two statements provide many thought provoking questions about reality and honesty that need to be addressed. War can lead to contrived falsehoods. False statements and deceit do not lead to solutions. Unless we are honestly looking for the truth, we are living a lie as Ted stated many times.

Symbols that Represent Ted's Life

The following artifacts are symbolic of Ted's life.

Vase

Some of the local people in Di Linh collected remnants of the war and turned them into useful works of art, tools, jewelry and souvenirs. One such item that Ted purchased from an artisan was a brass vase. It was crafted from a depleted 40 millimeter rocket shell (8 inches high and 3 inches in diameter). Ted gave this beautiful vase as a gift to his brother, Gary. The vase is now displayed at the Dayton International Peace Museum. It symbolizes a gift of beauty from something that was intended to kill and destroy. It is noteworthy that it was a 40 millimeter rocket shell that was used in the attack on the VNCS house the night Ted was killed. The transformation of a weapon of destruction into an object of beauty is an enduring symbol of peace and symbolic of Ted's life.

Vase made from a 40 mm rocket shell

Peace Poster

Ted hung a poster on the closet door in the bedroom where he was killed. The poster stated, "Suppose They Gave a War and Nobody Came." The peace poster is an ever-present reminder that his stand for peace and justice would not be impeded even at death. A replica of Ted's peace poster is on display at the Dayton International Peace Museum. See the poster in chapter 1 entitled, "Not Silenced in Death."

Guitar

Ted played his guitar and sang many folk ballads and peace songs including some of the Trinh Cong Son songs as they voice hope for peace through the universal language of music. His guitar songs and singing provided another engaging way to develop friendships. His guitar is now permanently displayed at the Dayton International Peace Museum.

Seeds

The seeds that Gary and Doug took to Di Linh from all of Ted's siblings were symbolic of their unity with him and the seeds of peace he had sown. They symbolize the many productive and life-giving characteristics of seeds as described in the scriptures.

Tree

The flowering Bougainvillea tree that Ted's brothers planted in Di Linh continues a family tradition of tree planting in memory of a deceased family member. The tree represents beauty, productivity and life giving qualities which are symbolic of Ted.

Glossary

Name	Definition
Amish	A group of traditionalist Christian church fellowships with Swiss Anabaptist origins. They are closely related to but distinct from Mennonite churches. The Amish are known for simple living, plain dress, and reluctance to adopt many conveniences of modern technology.
Anabaptist	A Christian who believes in delaying baptism until the candidate confesses his or her faith in Christ, as opposed to being baptized as an infant.
Di Linh	(Pronounced Zee Lin). A town in the Lam Dong Province in the Central Highlands of Vietnam with a population of over 155,000 as of 2003.
Hon Chong (The Rock)	Hon Chong also called The Rock is a group of massive Granite boulders along the coast just north of Nha Trang, Vietnam. They form a scenic wonder.
Khmer Rouge	A communist organization formed in Cambodia in 1970. They became a terrorist organization in 1975 when it captured Phnom Penh and created a government that killed an estimated three million people. They were defeated by Vietnamese troops but remained active until 1999.
Koho	Koho (pronounced caw-haw) is one of the tribal groups living in the highlands of Vietnam. It is a maternally influenced culture. Rituals, ceremonies and taboos are a way of life for many. Many are farmers.
Martyr	A person who suffers persecution and death for advocating or refusing to advocate a belief or cause as demanded by an external party.

Glossary

Name	Definition
Montagnard	The indigenous peoples of the Central Highlands of Vietnam. The term Montagnard means "mountain people" in French and is a carryover from the French colonial period in Vietnam.
Nonviolence	The use of peaceful means, not force, to bring about social and economic change.
Pakdy (Ven Pak)	Ted's wife, Pakdy, sometimes called Ven Pak was a child care volunteer through Asian Christian Service. She worked in Tuy Hoa, Vietnam.
Ram, Hydram or Hydraulic Ram	A system to pump a force of water to a higher level with a cyclic water pump driven by hydropower. It takes in water at one hydraulic head (pressure) and flow rate and outputs water at a higher hydraulic head and lower flow rate.
Tet Offensive	One of the largest military campaigns of the war in Vietnam, launched on January 30, 1968 by forces of the Viet Cong and North Vietnamese Army against South Vietnam, the United States, and their allies.
Viet Minh	A communist national independence coalition formed at Pac Bo on May 19, 1941. The Viet Minh initially formed to seek independence for Vietnam from the French Empire.
Vietnamization	A policy of the Nixon administration to end U.S. involvement in the war in Vietnam by equipping and training South Vietnam's forces and increasing their combat role while withdrawing U.S. troops.

About the Authors

Gary W. Studebaker

Gary is an older brother of Ted Studebaker. He served in Brethren Volunteer Service and International Voluntary Service as an agriculturalist in the country of Laos. He earned his teaching credentials at Manchester College (BS), California State University, L.A. (MA) and the University of Oregon (Ed.D). His career in special education included that of teacher, administrator and academic coach to special education teachers in the public schools in Southern California. He was a special education instructor at National University. His published books include biographies, poetry and the autism spectrum.

Douglas E. Studebaker

Doug grew up on the farm with his next older brother, Ted Studebaker. He prepared for a career in social work and business at Austin Peay State University (BS) and at UCLA (MSW/MBA). He had a lengthy social services career in developmental disabilities, home health care, hospice and employee counseling programs. Later he co-founded and managed Tibeca Home, an interior design and home furnishings business. Currently, Doug manages an Airbnb hospitality business, builds environmentally friendly tree houses and coaches high school pole vault athletes. He lives in Burlingame, California with his two daughters, Mackenzie and Chloe.

Bibliography

Aaker, Jerry. *A Spirituality of Service*. Middleton, WI: Pfeifer-Hamilton, 2012.

Church of the Brethren. "Ted Studebaker ABC News Story-YouTube." Church of the Brethren (Uploaded September 29, 2012). https://www.youtube.com/watch?v=vTqLmFS4yDs.

Civilian Public Service. "The Civilian Public Service Story—Living Peace in a Time of War." Mennonite Central Committee (May 15, 2011). http://civilianpublicservice.org/storycontinues.

Cribby, Phyllis. "Cribby Testimonial." Church of the Brethren Network (April 27, 1971) http://www.cob-net.org/ted/cribby.htm.

Dayton International Peace Museum. "Peace Heroes Walk." Dayton, OH: Dayton International Peace Museum, 2015, May 2, 2015.

Dull, Ralph. *Nonviolence is Not for Wimps*. Bloomington, IN: Xlibris Corporation, 2004.

Ediger, Max. *Friendships of Gold*. Bloomington, IN: Xlibris Corporation, 2001.

Egan, Nicole Weisensee. "How the Vietnam War's 'Napalm Girl' Is Finally Getting Her Scars Treated—43 Years Later." *People Magazine* (February 17, 2016). http://people.com/celebrity/how-the-napalm-girl-is-finally-getting-relief-from-pain/.

Ellsberg, Daniel. "Lying About Vietnam." *New York Times* (June 29, 2001). http://www.nytimes.com/2001/06/29/opinion/lying-about-vietnam.html

Engle, Steve. "Ted Studebaker in Vietnam." [CD]. Alexandria, PA: Dunkertown Records, (2005).

Friends with the Weather. "Brave Man from Ohio." (Andy Murray Cover), Live from Johnny's Speakeasy. (26 Jun 2016). https://www.youtube.com/watch?v=yTYf3Ahyndk

Gibran, Khalil. *The Prophet*. NY, New York: Alfred A. Knopf, 1969.

Handwerk, Brian. "Over a Quarter-Million Vietnam War Veterans Still Have PTSD." Smithsonian.com. (July 22, 2015) http://www.smithsonianmag.com/science-nature/over-quarter-million-vietnam-war-veterans-still-have-ptsd-180955997/.

Herod, Bill. "How the War in Afghanistan is Like the War in Viet-Nam." Unpublished paper, 2013.

Herod, Bill. "Ted." Unpublished paper, 1971.

Hunting, Jill. *Finding Pete*. Middletown, CT: Wesleyan University Press, 2009.

BIBLIOGRAPHY

Ip, Michael. "Looking Back: The End of the Vietnam War." ABC News (March 29, 2013). http://abcnews.go.com/blogs/headlines/2013/03/looking-back-the-end-of-the-vietnam-war/.

Jacobs, Harrison. "These 11 Gut-Wrenching Photos Show America's Devastating Legacy In Vietnam." *Business Insider* (August 5, 2014). http://www.businessinsider.com/paula-bronsteins-photos-of-disabled-agent-orange-vietnamese-2014-7.

Kempis, Thomas A. *Imitation of Christ*. New York: Grosset & Dunlap, 1966.

Kirchner, Shawn, et al. "Goodbye Still Night." North Manchester, IN: Manchester Church of the Brethren, 2014.

Lambert Reproductions. "Suppose they Gave a War—and Nobody Came." Posters. Washington, DC: Library of Congress Prints and Photographs Division, 1970.

MacDonald, Jacqueline, and Carmen Mendez. "The Cost of Cleaning up Unexploded Ordnance." www.rand.org. 2005.

Martin, Earl. *Reaching the Other Side*. New York: Crown, 1978.

Martin, Luke. *A Vietnam Presence*. Morgantown, PA: Masthof, 2016.

McNamera, Robert. *In Retrospect: The Tragedy and Lessons of Vietnam*. New York: Vintage, 1995.

Mishler, Mary Ann Studebaker. "Reflections About My Brother Ted." *Church of the Brethren Network*. http://www.cob-net.org/ted/maryann.htm.

Moore, Joy Hofacker. *Ted Studebaker: A Man Who Loved Peace*. Scottsdale, PA: Herald, 1987.

Murray, Andy and Terry Murray. "Brave Man From Ohio." [Recorded by Andy and Terry Murray]. On the CD album *River Still Running*.

Olson, Wyatt. "A New Approach to Ridding Vietnam of Unexploded Ordnance." *Stars and Stripes* (May 6, 2012). https://www.stripes.com/news/pacific/a-new-approach-to-ridding-vietnam-of-unexploded-ordnance-1.176497.

Parker, Don. "Life is Great. Yea," DVD, 2008.

Rawlings, Stewart. *The IVS Experience From Algeria to Vietnam*. Washington, DC: International Voluntary Service, 1992.

Royer, Howard. "A Dissenter from Despair." Messenger, Church of the Brethren General Board (1971) 4–5.

Sagnier, Thierry J. *The Fortunate Few*. Portland, OR: NCNM, 1915.

Studebaker, Gary W. "An Instrument of Peace." [CD, sung by Jackie Bissin]. On the album *Heroes and Friends*. Fullerton, CA: S1 Studios. (2015).

Studebaker, Gary W. "Everything is Copacetic." Anaheim, CA: TheSpectrumPress@gmail.com, 2015.

Studebaker, Gary W. and Amy Powell. *The Queen of Hearts, Zelma Louise Roth Studebaker*. Anaheim, CA: KNI, 1997.

Ulrich, Joel. "Family Reunion in Di Linh." Messenger, Church of the Brethren General Board (1998) 20–23.

Weidner, Keith. "To the Editor." *Troy Daily News*, July 24, 1971.

Yoder, Glee. *Passing on the Gift*. Elgin, IL: Brethren, 1978.

www.ingramcontent.com/pod-product-compliance
Lightning Source LLC
Chambersburg PA
CBHW061733270326
41928CB00011B/2220